STRATEGIES

FOR SAVING

YOUR SANITY ™

IN PARENTHOOD

Enjoy!
Mike Thomson

No Fluff... Just Answers

D1565831

by

Michael M. Thomson Ph.D.

Good Character Press, Inc.

Editor: Bob Kelly, WordCrafters, Inc.

Initial Reviewers: Carol Thomson, Ken Mangold

Illustration: John Uhrich, John McMenamin

Cover design: Robert DeVitis, DeVitis Design, Inc.

ISBN 1-883980-02-X

Although the author has exhaustively researched all sources to
ensure accuracy and completeness of the information con-
tained in this book, we assume no responsibility for errors,
inaccuracies, omissions or any other inconsistency herein.
Any slight against people or organizations is unintentional.
This book is not meant to replace advice of a professional
working with children and families. This book is designed to
provide competent and reliable information regarding the sub-
ject matter covered. Readers should consult a professional for
specific application to their individual problems. The author
and the publisher specifically disclaim any liability that is
incurred from the use or application of the contents of this
book.

To obtain information on Dr. Thomson's talks and additional
products, please call 1-800-290-2482.

For my wife, Carol, the absolute love of my life, and tied with the greatest gift God ever gave me – our two wonderful children, Christopher and Holly

It's not by chance God gave me two ears and one mouth. Thanks for allowing me to be a part of your life. You've taught me so much about the meaning of life, being a Dad and a husband, and the significance of being a role model for people I meet every day in life. I love you all.

Contents and Chapter Highlights

WHY YOU MUST LEARN A STRATEGY TO SAVE YOUR SANITY in the shortest possible time and become the greatest parent ever!...What in the world happened?... A few questions to consider... A hungry person comes to you... All we do is talk about the problems... My screaming falls on deaf ears... It's not the end of the world... Forward, march!

CREATING YOUR BLUEPRINT for parent success. This is it. The keys you've been waiting for. The oh-so-simple concepts to UNLEASHING THE POWER OF PARENTHOOD... The only people without problems are dead!... Unleashing the eight secrets to success as a parent... Six critical questions you MUST LEARN to save your sanity in parenthood.

WHY YOUR ATTITUDE MUST CHANGE, how to do it and what you'll get when you do. Choosing to think the way we want... Frustration levels are like shirt sizes... Same frustration, different responses... Our perceptions control our thoughts, actions and feelings...How we interpret events around us... Evaluating our present thoughts, actions and feelings... Key points to remember... Areas to practice and share... Typical problems – Dr. Mike's practical solutions.

MASTERING THE STRATEGY of turning all problems into opportunities. Unlocking your potential... How times have changed... Problems are opportunities in disguise... Using problems as opportunities for growth... Key points to remember... Areas to practice and share... Typical problems – Dr. Mike's practical solutions.

THREE SIMPLE CATEGORIES YOU MUST KEEP in your mind to save your sanity in parenthood... It's a tug of war!... Three simple categories to save your sanity... Three simple categories to teach your kids... At best, you have influence... Key points to remember... Areas to practice and share... Typical problems – Dr. Mike's practical solutions.

ACKNOWLEDGMENTS

The views used in this book have been influenced by the writings and training of many influential people in my career: William Glasser, M.D., founder of Reality Therapy, in which I am a certified reality therapist; Gary Applegate, Ph.D., author of *Happiness: It's Your Choice,* founder of the Skill Development Theory for Successful Change, and President of The Center For Productive Thinking in Los Angeles; Edward Ford, author of eleven books, including *Discipline for Home and School, Book One and Book Two;* the writings of Albert Ellis, Ph.D., founder of Rational Emotive Therapy, Aaron T. Beck, the father of cognitive therapy; and David Burns, M.D.

All of these people have cleared the path, as the early settlers did in this country, for many like myself to follow and expand upon ideas and strategies to help people. I owe all of them gratitude for their wisdom and teachings that widen my lenses as I continue to view the world of children, parents and the people with whom I come in contact daily.

My long-term exposure to the creative mind and talents of Dr. Gary Applegate is reflected in many of the ideas found in this book. My initial exposure to Dr. Applegate was through my training and subsequent certification in Reality Therapy. It launched a personal and professional friendship that continues to this day. Expanding on the basic concepts of Reality Therapy and Productive Thinking brought us together over the years to our work on many projects presenting these productive thinking skills to others around the world. Dr. Applegate wrote the forward to my first book *Who's Raising Whom?* applauding my application of Productive Thinking to successful parenting. Thanks Gary for being one of the most significant mentors in my life.

To my parents, Robert and Eileen, I owe everything. They were and continue to be the best of the best when it comes to parents. They've not only taught me the necessary skills in life, but modeled to me the skills I now teach and model to other parents and kids around the world. For these attributes, I thank them so very much.

Mark Twain could have had me in mind when he said, *"When I was fourteen it seemed to me that my parents did not know anything. I could hardly stand to have them around. By the time I was twenty-one, I was impressed at how much they had learned."* Mom and Dad, you did good!

To my brother Brent, all of my memories of childhood are filled with the days of hockey, camping, movies together, fighting as bear cubs, and the friendship that continues to this day. Brent had the good fortune of doing his doctoral work at The Ohio State University, in conjunction with a Drug Free Schools project I was on.

Throughout our professional careers, we've had many discussions concerning this book and related projects. I'm grateful for all of his wisdom and support. He models naturally what many people search a lifetime for. Thanks, Brent.

I also want to acknowledge Ken Mangold, my business partner and one of the key players in making this book a reality. There's not enough paper to hold my thoughts about you. You're always such a positive person to be around. You keep pushing me to stay positive, to keep writing, speaking, and creating new products, in order to make this world a better place. You're always there for me. Thanks so much for all of your support and friendship over the years.

Others I wish to acknowledge include the professors in my life who carried me through my educational travels. Dr. Rhea Das and Dr. Janice Kuldau, from the University of Wisconsin-Superior, welcomed me into the university world with open and supportive arms of encouragement to gather as much academic exposure as possible in the pursuit of my bachelor's degree in psychology.

Dr. Tim Hatfield, from Winona State University in Minnesota, provided me with the opportunity to expand my thinking skills and to incorporate my beliefs into the alcohol and drug treatment fields. His wit and ever-present assistance were greatly appreciated in my Master of Science training.

Dr. Joseph Quaranta, Jr. opened the door for my doctoral work in the Department of Education Theory and Practice at The Ohio State University. Dr. Quaranta was not only my advisor, but a terrific mentor who supervised my internship toward licensure as a psychologist. He's filled with a tremendous amount of wit, humor and intelligence that makes my association with him so very special to this day. What a great guy!

One last person to acknowledge: Dr. Robert Niven. My experience at The Mayo Clinic, in the Department of Psychology and Psychiatry, virtually widened my lenses to the multitude of behaviors people exhibit and the treatment techniques to help them. Dr. Niven not only allowed me, but encouraged me to continually increase my education and understanding while refining my skills and, as a result, became an important role model of professional techniques and strategies in working with people.

I owe all these people so much for their personal and professional knowledge and skills that helped build my character into what it is today. Thank you all so very much.

AUTHOR'S NOTE

Dear Reader,

Have you been feeling like you've been shot to a different planet compared to when you grew up? Well guess what…you have been! Remember the days on what I now call the "old planet" when parents told kids to listen and they did, to be quiet and they were, behave and they did? Do you wish we still had some of those "old days" here again? Well let's face it, you're not alone. We all do. If you just look around today, you'll see and hear a lot of parents ready to scream out loud. Welcome to the world of parenthood.

Now here's the question of the hour…Are you interested in learning a strategy to save your sanity? Or, at least save what's left of it?

Your desire for results has brought you to this book. Congratulations for making a commitment to seeking out new knowledge on this amazing journey called parenthood.

My goal in writing *Strategies For Saving Your Sanity™ In Parenthood* is twofold: first, to fire you up inside by unleashing what I think is the hidden power within parenthood; and second, to provide you with practical advice for turning your energy into positive simple steps that will lead you forward in your life.

I wrote this book for those with an "education on the go" mentality. No fluff…just answers. I know we're all busier than ever and, at the same time, concerned about the welfare of our children. This isn't going to be like a drive-up parenting window, but rather a buffet of new ideas for you to incorporate into your present skill level as a parent.

You'll find the advice in this book easily digestible in just minutes a day. My experience over the years has taught me that you'll find yourself coming back to this book throughout parenthood for a "refresher" from time to time. Read and re-read the pages until they curl right up!

Here are four simple steps to getting the most out of the book: 1) read a few pages at a time; 2) sit back and reflect on what you've read; 3) share your reflections with others, if you so choose, or keep a journal for yourself of what you're getting out of this book; and 4) practice using the new concepts learned in your daily life.

I've been convinced over the years that changing what we're doing in life is preceded by stepping back and rethinking about our own thoughts first. Rethinking about our role as a parent. Rethinking about our children. And finally, rethinking about the world around us.

Last but not least, thank you for giving me the opportunity to share these pages of advice with you.

If you use even one of these suggestions, you'll be taking one step beyond where you were yesterday. And it may just be that step that will save your sanity!

I look forward to personally meeting you one day on your journey through parenthood.

Michael M. Thomson
"Dr. Mike"

Chapter 1

Nobody Gave Us a Manual!

WHY YOU MUST LEARN A STRATEGY TO SAVE YOUR SANITY in the shortest possible time and become the greatest parent ever!

"I talk and talk and none of the kids listen to me. I feel like I'm losing my mind. They look at me and just shrug their shoulders when I ask them to listen. I can't stand it anymore."
—Parent of four-, seven-, and nine-year-olds

"Every time I think I'm going to get a break, he cries again. Doesn't this kid know when to sleep and when to stay awake? If I make it through this it will be a miracle. This is so frustrating!"
—Parent of a two-year-old

"You take a privilege away and they say 'so,' or 'doesn't bother me,' or the classic 'whatever.' My kids tell me 'you're not the boss of me' on a regular basis. This is nuts! I'm counting the days until they're 18!"
—Parent of ten-, twelve-, and sixteen-year-olds

"My kids don't see school as that important. They bring home very little, if any, homework. Getting them to do it is another thing. Some days it's an all-out war to get them up for school. Coming home on time is another thing. They say they can't wait until they're 18—neither can I!"
—Parent of thirteen- and seventeen-year-olds

"I fight with my kids to get them to bed. I fight with my kids to get them up in the morning. They're impossible. They blame everything on others, including me. They never take responsibility for anything. How do you teach them responsibility and good decisions?"
—Parent of ten-, twelve-, and fourteen-year-olds

Can you relate to any of these? Have you ever told your relatives, friends, or co-workers about some of the poor choices either your kids or other kids are making today? Have you been in discussions with others about the attitude of kids today versus when you were growing up? You know as well as I do that they'll look you straight in the eye and say something like, *"Well, I wouldn't put up with that! You mean to tell me that you allow them to do that?"* leaving you feeling like a flop!

"What's wrong with me?" "Why can't I get my kids to act the way those other kids do?" "Why can't I control them like my parents controlled me?" "Maybe the 'good old days' really were the 'good old days' after all?" Sound familiar?

In regard to this, have you ever heard parents say something like: *"I can't stand it anymore." "My kids act like such jerks." "They're so lazy." "I don't think they'll ever learn to be responsible?"* Have you ever observed parents excessively yelling, screaming, threatening, spanking and lecturing their kids?

On the flip side, have you ever heard kids say something like *"So." "Whatever." "Oh—that's cool." "Fine, just fine," "You can ground me for the rest of my life because I'm not going to change?"* Have you ever seen or heard any of these? Are they driving you crazy? Are you ready to scream? Are you looking for the receipt for the kids so you can return them? Are you looking for the answer? You're not alone!

First question: **Would you be interested in learning a strategy to save your sanity?** Second question: **Have you already lost your sanity?** In this book, I'll tell you how and when you lost your sanity and, better yet, I'll teach you how to get it back!

I believe you must learn a strategy to save your sanity in the shortest possible time and become the greatest parent ever! Why? Because your kids are depending on you. And because I'm depending on you!

Questioning or even losing our sanity as a parent didn't happen overnight—the world gradually changed around us. The world of parenthood is tough at best! I mean think of this: you need a license to fish, a license to hunt, a license to drive a car, a license to get married—but when it comes to parenthood, no license is required.

There are no classes to take, no sure-fire tricks to learn and no Cliff notes to grab at the last minute like I used to do in high school. Advice from everyone—from our parents, grandparents, friends, co-workers, and even strangers—varies from the reasonably sane to the ridiculous.

Nobody gave us a manual with our children. In fact, you get more instructions with a new microwave than you do with a child!

What in the world happened?

The frustration that accompanies raising children has been increasing steadily over the years, and has now brought many a parent to their knees begging for help. Kids show widespread lack of respect towards parents and other adults, and even to their own peers. Many kids are treating their parents like dirt. They verbally abuse them, swear at them, threaten them, and sometimes physically fight with them.

Their "demandingness," in the form of a "me" attitude or the *"I-don't-care-about-anyone-but-myself"* attitude, is sometimes overshadowed by the ever popular, *"I-can't-wait-until-I'm-eighteen-then-I-can-do-what-I-want"* attitude. Other parents are wondering whether their child's middle name is **"get me, buy me, take me, give me!"** They are so ungrateful. So disrespectful. So demanding.

It's no wonder many a parent has told me that the promised joys of parenthood are turning into real nightmares! Parent burnout is on the rise, and the white flag, or *"I-give-up"* attitude, seems to be quite frequently waved around nowadays by many parents.

Kids may be saying they can't wait until they're eighteen, but many a parent has told me they, too, can't wait till that day arrives! The feelings, they say, are mutual. Now I understand why parents buy their kids luggage as a graduation gift! I wonder if that says anything about the changing attitude in this country?

I've lectured to more than a million people throughout the world, and keep hearing the same comments from parents:

"Kids don't listen today."
"I want them to shut up when I say shut up!"
"Kids are so irresponsible."
"Why ground them? They make life miserable for you."
"You can't take away privileges from teenagers."
"Kids do whatever they want to."
"How do you get them to make good decisions?"
"I wouldn't have been able to sit down for weeks if I had talked to my parents that way."
"How do you get kids to change when they don't want to?"
"There's nothing we can do!"
"We need to get tougher with them."
"I'll be damned if some kid of mine is going to run my life or this house!"
"Maybe we should just let them do what they want to."

On the flip side, the comments heard over and over from kids today are:
"Parents don't listen."
"Parents don't give us any responsibility."
"Parents figure that when we turn eighteen we magically develop responsibility—what a joke."
"My parents don't even care about me."

"They do and say what they want, why can't I?"
"Parents just don't understand."
"Do as I say, not as I do—that's a joke."
"They yell and scream at me, and then tell me not to scream at them."
"Everybody thinks we have such a kid problem today; it's not that we have a kid problem, but that we have an adult problem."
"We do as much or as little as our parents allow us to get away with."
"My parents want to trust me, but they never allow me to earn that trust."
"Parents think it's the end of the world if a kid wears an earring, dresses funky, talks weird or listens to rock music— they're so wrong."
"My parents are really crabby all the time."
"Parents never let us choose what we want to think, or choose what we want to do—they're so controlling, I can't stand it."
"Parents tell me to listen, but they keep cutting in on me."
"Parents want me to tell them everything about my life, but they tell me to never mind when I ask about their life."

These comments point to the fact that we're having problems in our relationships between parents and their kids, and kids and their parents. You don't have to be a rocket scientist to just feel the frustration when you read through these.

Much of the research on the family over the years has focused on what's going wrong, centering in on problems occurring within families, rather than on what constitutes a healthy family.

Turn on the television set and listen to the nightly news, and you can see that peoples' interests are generally directed more toward what's going wrong with the world and catching people in the act of being bad, rather than focusing on "good news" stories. The focus appears to be more on sickness than on health.

That's why this book will focus on what we "can do" to correct the negative aspects of today's families. We'll address each and every one of these statements of concern. Knowing there are concerns from both sides is one thing; knowing what to do about them is another.

A few questions to consider…

Let me ask you a few questions. Would you be interested in learning how to teach your children to be responsible for what they do, what they think, and how they ultimately feel? I mean really being responsible for not only their good choices, but also their poor choices? Would you be interested in learning a strategy to teach your children how to make good decisions, so they're less at risk of making the poor choices that lead to drinking, drugging, sexual promiscuity, delinquent behavior, along with generally disruptive behavior?

What about learning how to teach your children to take effective control of their own lives so they have that internal power to resist negative influences from their peers and others? How about a simple strategy for getting them to do their homework, clean up their messes, use good manners, earn trust, to do their chores, clean their rooms, make their beds, throw down the dirty laundry, go to bed on time, or get up in the morning without being screamed at?

Would it be less stressful if they just did one of these? What if they did all of them? I can see it now; your kids would be dialing 911 because you dropped to the floor in shock! (At least I hope they'd grab the phone and dial the number)

I'm continually asked by audiences for the answers to these very questions in the ever-frustrating quest for the key to parenthood. In this book, you'll receive the answers to these questions, as well as to other frequent and frustrating problems.

A hungry person comes to you...

Here's the philosophy on which this book is based:

You can give others a fish and feed them for the evening; or, you can teach them how to fish so they can feed themselves for the rest of their lives.

As a parent, you're hungry for answers. I can give you the "pat" answers to many frequently asked questions, but that would be giving you a fish and only solving the problem temporarily. It's like putting mud in a crack in the dam. It will hold for a while, but for how long?

I believe that if I teach you the skills on how to use *The Eight Areas Of The Power Of Productive Choices,* along with *The Six Critical Questions,* in every problem in life, it will help you both personally and professionally for the rest of your life.

Think about this. Our kids come into the world like the hungry man looking for food. It seems to me our primary goal as parents is to prepare our children for the world they're entering. That preparation occurs while they're living with us, and represents our best attempt to enable them to live successfully when they eventually leave home.

That preparation should ready them for all the stresses of daily living, and all the ups and downs they'll experience. In a sense, we're better off teaching our children "how to fish," so they can feed themselves for the rest of their lives.

Many times, however, our kids come wanting us to solve **"their problems"** and make **"their decisions,"** and as a result, accept **"their responsibility"** for **"their choices"** and **"their feelings."** In doing so, we're only giving them a fish, or problem solving **"for them"** every time they run into difficulty.

But in the long run, does this really help? Does it become a problem for us and for them when we step in to help? When does it get to this point? Does it become a pattern, where every time they have a problem, or a decision to make, they run to someone "out there" for the solution?

You know and I know a boatload of adults who can't make decisions on their own. They're what I call the "recovering adolescent" group, who are 30, 40, 50, or even 60 years old, and still wanting others to take control of their decisions as well as their lives.

I think you and I both know the problem isn't theirs alone. The problem is that nobody taught them the productive thinking skills they needed to learn, in order to take effective control of their own lives. Who do you think are the teachers of problem solving and decision making skills? Yeah, you're right—we, as parents. But wait a minute, who taught us these skills, and was what we were taught the right method for today's kids?

With the above philosophy as our inspiration, I can take you beyond the traditional approaches to parenthood that I believe are problem-solving and crisis-driven in nature. **I'll begin to teach you the success-oriented skills required so that control over one's own life is where it belongs—in the hands of the person with the problem.**

All we do is talk about the problems…

Mark Twain once said, *"Everybody talks about the weather, but nobody does anything about it."* A similar observation might be made about parenthood. Have you ever-heard people say:

"Kids nowadays are going nowhere in life."

"I can't even begin to imagine what it must be like to grow up in today's society."

"There's nothing you can do with these kids nowadays, just let them do what they want. The heck with them."

It seems to me that everybody talks about the problems we're having, but too many people do little or nothing to increase their skills to resolve them. Everyone has an opinion and expresses feelings about the problems we have in today's society and with today's children, but few people are practicing a new strategy to effectively deal with daily problems.

I think it's because a new strategy requires hard work and determination. A new strategy requires you to go beyond where you are and begin to increase your own skills. It requires thinking differently about yourself, not only in the sense of who you are, but also what you want in life.

It requires thinking about the world around you, including those who are significant to you. It requires an evaluation of your present skills as a parent. It also requires an evaluation of where you want to be as a parent from this point forward.

Because you've chosen to read this book, I believe you've decided, "*I must put new information into my life that will increase my present skill level as a parent. The more information I have, the more choices I'll have and the more skills I'll have. The more skills I have as a parent, the more secure I'll feel.*" And I believe this new attitude will take you to a different level than where most parents are.

When I became a parent, it seemed everybody had "the" answer that worked with every situation. *"This is what you need to do when this happens."* Oh sure! Well, it didn't work that well for me. As a new parent, I kept thinking, "Maybe I'm deformed in some way. Maybe I was dipped in the shallow end of the parenting gene pool! Maybe I wasn't meant to parent. Maybe I need some new skills to help me through this trying time." Thank goodness I've changed—for the better!

My screaming falls on deaf ears

Right now, you may be making certain choices to "correct" your child that seem to be working. They may include excessive yelling, screaming, verbal threatening, or possibly even spanking, to name just a few.

You may also be aware that those choices, even though they may temporarily work, carry with them consequences—such as the child doing what you say "only" when you use "force." These choices can quickly lead your kids from disliking you to hating you, for controlling or overpowering them. They can quickly become afraid of you. These choices can also quickly destroy any chance at a relationship with your kids.

The problem with us having a "more-power-than-you attitude" leads us into a no-win situation fast. It might work when they're little because, face it, you are bigger than they are. But in the long run, it frustrates the dickens out of both of you. And it teaches nothing other than that someone with more power is in control. Yuck! It unfortunately also sets up a belief in the child's mind that he or she is a "bad child."

Now let's get things straight right up front; these choices don't make anyone a "bad person." They just mean someone's making a poor choice at the time. Making this simple, yet powerful change in your thinking is one of the keys to saving your sanity. You'll begin to view problems as a springboard for discussion regarding the variety of choices to be made "next time" a similar situation may occur.

It's not the end of the world…

Please understand that it's not the end of the world if your kids or you have made poor choices in the past. You can't change the past. But, you do have control over changing your thoughts and actions from this point forward. Developing an *"I have control over me"* and *"I have control over changing myself"* attitude will make a significant difference in your life.

If as a parent you ever find yourself feeling guilty about some of the "poor choices" you made in the past, remember you were using the best choices you knew of at the time to deal with the frustration at hand. Before blaming yourself totally, think about how you've been influenced over the years. Who taught you how to solve the daily problems of living? Where did you learn how to deal with problems? From your parents? On your own? Through trial and error? From television?

This book is a collection of many years of personal and professional experiences, working directly and indirectly with millions of parents and kids, presenting seminars, fielding questions on radio and television talk shows, and being raised by my own children, Christopher and Holly.

As I step back and reflect, I'm really fortunate to have had the experiences with all the people I've listened to over the years. These people and their stories have given me a wealth of information to draw from. My kids, and other kids around the world, have taught me not only what they like but also quite frankly what they hate in parents.

On the flip side, the parents have taught me not only how to parent but how not to parent. So, the bottom line is that it's not by chance that God gave me two ears and one mouth; as a result, this book becomes the mouthpiece for my many years of experiences.

Forward, march…

With these changes in mind and obstacles to overcome, I hope you'll find the strategies suggested in this book beneficial in "saving your sanity," and at the same time, produce responsible, capable young people of good character.

This book is based on reality. It's not going to be research-based, or on a bunch of surveys or theories. It's full of practical common sense. I really hope your kids and you can enjoy it together and profit from the information. I'm going to provide you with a practical strategy to help you, not only as a parent, but in all areas of your life, both personal and professional.

Hopefully, you'll begin to see changes in how you choose to think about yourself and the world around you. I'm not going to offer a standard set of parenthood rules, but provide you with a specific **productive thinking strategy** for dealing with a wide range of issues that will come up in parenthood. In other words, I hope to give you "good old" common sense information.

I'm also going to provide you with the specific skills to rethink your role as a parent, to rethink your kids' choices, and to learn to take more effective control of yourself in your role and responsibility as a parent. If you're ready, then welcome to the world of parenthood, and welcome to going beyond general information on parenthood and learning a practical strategy that will save your sanity. Forward, march!

Chapter 2

The Eight Areas of "The Power of Productive Choices" and "The Six Critical Questions"

CREATING YOUR BLUEPRINT for parental success. This is it. The keys you've been waiting for. The oh-so-simple concepts to UNLEASHING THE POWER OF PARENTHOOD

Effective from this point forward, your kids are all done blaming you or others for their problems. No more *"Thanks for putting me to bed early," "You grounded me," "You took away my toys, my car, my stereo, it's not fair," "The reason I hit my brother/sister is that they hit me first," "The teacher gave me a bad grade." "The teacher put me in detention or in-school-suspension," "The cop gave me a ticket." "The boss fired me." "The coach kicked me off the team,"* or the ever popular, *"Everybody else was doing it, it was peer pressure!"*

I've had it! I'm so sick of this "blame it on others" victimhood mentality I could scream! We need to change this mentality—and change it fast. And I don't want us to lose our cool trying to get it accomplished. But, bottom line, I think it's time we step up to the plate and confront this mentality head-on.

As a parent, you're all done yelling, screaming or raising your voice excessively to your kids. Wouldn't this be great? No more going nuts. No more arguments. No more threatening. I'm going to teach you a strategy to save your sanity. As we go along, you'll learn *The Eight Areas of "The Power of Productive Choices."*

Notice I use the word "Power" in my description. I believe that if you put the skills I teach you in this book into your life as a parent, you'll begin to have incredible power. I truly believe this power is going to be your ticket to changing your life as a parent. It's also going to be the ticket for providing your kids with the necessary skills to take effective control of their lives.

We'll also examine *The Six Critical Questions* that will tremendously change your life as a parent. These simple questions will bring life into parenthood. They'll bring life into your kids. They'll make your role as a parent so much simpler. You'll see these questions in a mini-poster format throughout the book, as a reference piece that will prove to be invaluable.

I'm also going to recommend solutions for many typical problems that arise in the parent-child relationship.

At the end of each chapter, I'll present a variety of typical problems and practical solutions for parents of pre-school, elementary, middle and high school age kids. It's one thing to read theories, but it's another thing to use actual examples. I learn from examples. I think you will too.

The only people without problems are DEAD!

Because you have children, you will have problems. **We need to recognize that the only people without problems are dead!** That's right, dead! Because you're reading this book, you're obviously not dead. So welcome to parenthood and to a life filled with problems—problems I believe can be looked at in a whole new way.

Welcome to a strategy I call *The Power of Productive Choices,* that allow problems to be viewed as opportunities for growth. Welcome to a strategy that will save your sanity. Welcome to a strategy that will do the same for your kids and their kids to come.

Knowing all people have problems should relieve some of your stress. Notice I said "some." As with all problems, you can reduce the degree of stress and frustration you experience, but you can't totally eliminate it.

I worry about all those books, seminars, and tapes that claim they can teach people they can totally eliminate stress. Not me! I want a better way. A more efficient way. A way that gives me control over my own life. A way that doesn't rely totally on other people.

I want to not only relieve your stress and frustration with parenthood and other life hassles, but to **EMPOWER you with a whole new set of thinking skills and more effective action skills** to deal with the daily problems of living. These new skills will provide you with more alternatives for similar problems that may arise later. The more effective skills you have in dealing with problems, the more secure you'll feel when other problems arise. Feeling secure and in control is what we all want.

Unleashing the EIGHT SECRETS to success as a parent

1. Thinking from "Reaction" to **Rethinking**
2. Rethinking from "Problems" to **Opportunities**
3. Rethinking from "Out of Control" to **Control**
4. Rethinking from "No Choice" to **Choices**
5. Rethinking from "Controlling" to **Relationship**
6. Rethinking from "Wants" to **Needs**
7. Rethinking from "External" to **Internal**
8. Rethinking from "Outcome" to **Process**

1. The first area of *The Power of Productive Choices* is changing your
    thinking from "reaction" to **Rethinking.** We've all reacted to problem
    situations. Someone has said or done something and we chose to react.
    You notice I said, "chose to react." In my experience, when we choose to
    react, the problem, whatever it is or whoever it involves, has got you!

    Your focus is on "out there." You just lost control. When you lose
    control, you react. When you react, you might raise your voice, and say
    and/or do things you might not normally say or do. And, to top it off,
    you begin to think in ways you might not normally think.

    In today's society, we're unfortunately so conditioned to react to a
    problem with a typical thought, like *"What am I going to do?"* I don't
    want you "to do" anything. That's the problem! We all want to "react"
    and "do something" to stop the frustration.

    We'll show you, in a later chapter, that productive people go against
    the grain of common sense thinking, choosing to step back and use the
    power of Rethinking in all problem situations. Thinking clearly about the
    problem and not reacting to it is the key here.

2. The second area of *The Power of Productive Choices* is rethinking from
    "problems" to **Opportunities.** Having problems in your life isn't the end
    of the world. We've already seen that the only people without problems
    are dead.

    So what makes the difference between people who choose to stay stuck with problems and those who choose to rethink them? Notice I use two significant words here, "Choose" and "Rethink."

In a later chapter, we'll look at how productive people choose to view the world as a smorgasbord of choices they can make. They know these choices then become opportunities to turn their problems around. They know they have the power and the control to rethink and make the right choices in life, even when no one's watching. And that's the true test of a person of good character.

3. The third area of *The Power of Productive Choices* is rethinking from "out of control" to **Control.** Have you ever "lost it"? Have you ever said or done something and, moments later, regretted it? The real question is how long we've stayed in a negative mood about something we really had no control over.

    In a later chapter, we'll see that productive people choose to step back, rethink and separate their problem situations into three simple categories: what they can control; what they can influence; and what they have no control over.

4. The fourth area of *The Power of Productive Choices* is rethinking from "no choice" to **Choices.** There are three types of people I've met in my travels around the world. When problems arise, they make significantly different choices.

    The first person is the one who "quits and leaves," who sees himself or herself as stuck, as having no choices, as having no control, and who chooses to quit and leave the problem situation.

    The second person is the one I'm really after in my talks around the country. These are the ones who choose to "quit and stay," to stay stuck, and wait for the world around them to change. They become the whiners, the pouters, the complainers, and the ain't-it-awful group. Do you know some of these people?

    The third person is the one who chooses to "stay and rethink," who teaches and models the principles found throughout this book. These people rethink, turn problems into opportunities, focus on choices they have control over, focus on building relationships with people, focus on meeting their needs with people, and believe parenting is a multitude of process steps.

5. The fifth area of *The Power of Productive Choices* is rethinking from "controlling" to **Relationship.** The biggest issue that comes up in any relationship is the issue of control. One person wants something and the other person doesn't always provide it. Therein lies the problem and therein lies the solution, as we'll see in more detail in a later chapter.

The more you and I attempt to control another person's thoughts, actions or feelings, the more "out of control" we become. Just try forcing your thoughts, actions and feelings on other people. It's like trying to shove a horse's head in the water in an attempt to get it to drink. Good luck!

We can't force that horse to drink, even though we lead it to the water, but we'll show you how to put lots of salt in its oats. In the same way, we as parents can learn great ways to influence our kids to make the right choices in life, even when we're not around. Before you as a parent can make a difference, your kids need to know you care. Children don't care how much you know until they know how much you care.

6. The sixth area of *The Power of Productive Choices* is rethinking from "wants" to **Needs.** We all want what we want when we want it. These aren't only wants we have for ourselves but also for our children, in how they should think, act or feel. For example, we want our kids to be happy, productive and responsible.

    Later, we'll show that productive people know it's impossible to always give others what they want. Productive people change their focus and look at providing a need-fulfilling environment, plus the skills to meet those needs in all areas of life. These psychological needs are what draw your children toward you, and are also what draw them away from you.

7. The seventh area of *The Power of Productive Choices* is rethinking from "external" to **Internal.** So many of us have been conditioned to believe that, if we can just find some "outside" stimulus to motivate others, this is the key to somehow magically get kids to think, act or feel the way we want them to.

    The discipline approach grew out of this belief system. Unfortunately, this and other controlling approaches have fostered a wrong belief that "we" have more power, control and choice than the person with the problem behavior does.

    In a later chapter, we'll show you how to teach and model the "internal" skills your kids need to learn at any age to become productive members of society, despite what's going on or not going on around them. I want everyone to get off the "victimhood" bandwagon and take effective control of their own lives.

8. The eighth and final area of *The Power of Productive Choices* is rethinking from "outcome" to **Process.** It's no news flash that we live in a quick-fix society that wants everything solved by noon tomorrow, at the latest. You and I both know that just thinking about the outcomes in life will actually lead to more frustration, because these outcomes aren't

always within our control. Later, we'll look at how to step back and rethink that problems need to be handled in little "baby steps."

Six Critical Questions you MUST LEARN to save your sanity in parenthood

Insert the problem here.

WHO owns the
PROBLEM?

WHO owns the
RESPONSIBILITY?

WHO made the
DECISIONS?

WHO has the
POWER?

WHO has the
CONTROL?

WHO makes the
CHOICES?

CHARACTER

©Michael M. Thomson Ph.D. 1995

The next area I want you as a parent to begin rethinking in is what I call *The Six Critical Questions*. We sell a colorful mini-poster and wall poster people are using all around the world, to remind them of these simple steps in their daily lives. Putting this poster up in a visible location will keep everybody on the same page when dealing with the daily problems of living.

I hope you'll find this chart very useful in your journey through parenthood. It will serve as the backdrop for the information that follows. You'll find yourself referring back to this chart in your self-discovery and discussions with others, regarding any of the suggestions we make in this book.

Go ahead, try it out. Think of any problem you might be having and work your way through the questions. Using them in your life will keep you focused in the right direction. Using them with others will influence them to think differently. I think you'll find them invaluable.

The first part of the poster has the statement, "Insert the problem here." Notice the hand on the left. As you point to the problem, three fingers point directly back at you. This is an important visual reminder for you and your kids, pointing out who really has the power, control and choices in solving the problems of life. Those who choose "victimhood" will quickly want to point all the fingers and the thumb to "out there" as the problem.

We have a better alternative that will empower you and your kids. Having used this approach for years, I'm convinced you can take any problem you or others are experiencing and work your way down through these questions to find the correct solution.

1. The first question is **"Who Owns the Problem?"** I believe that in 98 percent of the problem situations in life, it's critical to avoid becoming a

problem solver for others, but rather a teacher of better alternative choices to take effective control of life's daily problems.

If you choose to become a problem solver, it unfortunately will create a perception in the other person's mind of you owning the problem, as well as owning the solution to the problem. Yuck! This is immediately going to put you in a burnout position in life. What you'll learn in this book is how to immediately step back, rethink, and become a teacher and a model of efficient choices to your kids.

Let's quickly think about a list of potential problems you might run into as a parent: getting your kids out of bed; getting them to go to bed; having a negative attitude; not coming in on time; not doing homework; using alcohol or other drugs; being lied to; not doing their chores around the house, etc.

"Who Owns the Problem?" You're right! They do. Why do we, as parents, feel we own these problems? And why do we allow ourselves to take them on?

From this point forward, you need to begin the process of saving your sanity by stepping back and rethinking what part of the problem you own. By doing this, you'll also begin to understand what part of the problem the other person owns. Do not, and I repeat, do not take on problems that aren't yours—*if* you want to save your sanity!

2. The second question is **"Who Owns the Responsibility?"** What I want you to do is to immediately step back, rethink, and ask yourself what part of the problem are you responsible for? If you decide you own either all or part of the problem, then you need to take control by admitting it and making the appropriate changes in order to reconcile the problem.

If you believe you don't own either all or part of the problem, then you need to ask yourself what part of it the other person's responsible for. If you find the other person is responsible for either all or part of the problem, then you need to focus on what you have control over in this situation, which is you, and how you choose to think, act and feel.

You can then choose to turn this into a learning opportunity, for both of you. Asking these first two questions, *"What part of the problem am I responsible for?"* and *"What part of the problem is the other person responsible for?"* will immediately relieve you of taking on other people's problems and/or responsibility.

When you really step back and rethink about such problems as getting out of bed, going to bed, having a negative attitude, not coming in on time, not doing homework, using alcohol or other drugs, being lied to, or not doing household chores, you can start to understand that it's really stressful for us to take on these responsibilities for our kids.

And remember, you're reading this book because you're interested in saving your sanity, not losing it. What you will learn is how to put the responsibility for the problem where it belongs.

3. The third question is **"Who Made the Decisions?"** It's critical for us to step back and rethink about the decisions made in any problem situation. You need to begin by asking yourself: "Did I make the decision in this problem situation? Did I make the decision to not get up on time, not go to bed on time, have a negative attitude, not do the assigned homework, to use alcohol or other drugs, to lie or to not do the chores?"

   I hope it's becoming crystal clear by now that you and I as parents are not responsible for the decisions our kids make. They own the problem. They own the responsibility. If you believe that, in the problem situation you're dealing with, you're the one who made the decision, then you own the problem, the responsibility and the decision.

   Admitting this to your child shows you're human and do make mistakes, but that you own up to your mistakes. If, on the other hand, you believe you don't either own part or all of the decisions, then you need to ask yourself what part of the decision the other person's responsible for.

   You'll learn in this book that working your way through the first three of *The Six Critical Questions* will immediately relieve you of taking on other people's problems, responsibility and decisions.

4. The fourth question is **"Who Has the Power?"** Step back and figure out what power you have over this problem situation. Also ask yourself what power the other person has over this situation. Your kids have the internal power to get out of bed in the morning, get into bed at night, clean up their attitude, come in on time, do their homework, avoid alcohol or other drugs, not lie, and do their chores around the house.

   The power to rethink about problems and all the strategies for saving your sanity alluded to in this book come from within yourself.

   We'll outline the skills to put into your own life first. By doing this, and in fact just learning *The Six Critical Questions,* will create a sense of power in your life that I think you'll really appreciate. Learning and developing these skills provides you tremendous power to tackle the everyday problems in parenthood and in life.

5. The fifth question is **"Who Has the Control?"** This is where it's critical for us to step back and rethink about who really has the control here. Do I have it in this problem situation? Does the other person involved have it? Staying with our short list of problems listed above, you can quickly see who has the control—your kids do. All you have is influence over them and, sometimes, let's face it, no control over whether or not they do as they should.

We'll show you how to separate all problems into three simple categories of control, influence, and no control, and to teach and model this to your kids. Doing this simple step will immediately lower your stress level, and help you begin to focus in a whole new way about the daily problems you run into. This question and the skills you'll learn in the chapter on *Control* will literally save your sanity ten times over!

6. The sixth question is **"Who Makes the Choices?"** Step back and ask yourself what choices you made as a parent in this situation. Then ask yourself what choices the other person involved in this problem made.

    Keeping your questions focused on the concept of choices makes you, and your kids, aware that you know that people have the power and control to make both good and poor choices—all the time.

    My wife and I have always taught our kids that, if they choose not to get out of bed or into bed on time, not clean up their attitudes, not come in on time, not do homework, to use alcohol or other drugs, to lie, or to not do their household chores, then we'll step in and make choices "we" have 100 percent control over.

    By stepping in, we'll be closing the First National Bank of Mom and Dad, the ride service will be shut down, the privileges they once enjoyed will be stopped, and their lives will change.

    We've made it very clear to our kids that we'd never ground them, never take away their allowance money, or their privileges—their poor choices would. Wow! What a switch in our thinking. And, as a result, what a strategy to save our sanity!

Now here's a great wrap-up story on this chapter I want to share with you. I'll never forget when I first came out with the *Six Critical Questions* poster. My parents were in the audience, proud as peacocks. Like everyone else, they received a mini-poster of these questions to follow along during my program.

After the talk, my parents and I went out for coffee. My mother laid the chart on the table and said, *"Michael, when you were growing up in our home, were there times we took on problems that were actually yours?"* Can you picture this question being asked of you?

Well, I remember lowering my head, rolling my eyes, and saying something quietly like, *"Don't take this wrong, but yes. As parents there were times when you not only took on my problems, but my responsibility, my decisions, my power, my control and my choices."*

At first, I could see that my parents felt pretty bad about what I said. They looked like they'd done something wrong. I quickly explained to them that, over the years, I've come to believe that EVERY PARENT takes on their kids' problems, responsibility, decisions, power, control and choices, at various times in their lives.

It doesn't mean we're bad or even defective parents. We're all human. We've all done this to some degree or another. In fact, if you really think about it, if we don't take these areas on when our kids come out of the womb, they'd die!

The "gazillion-dollar" question I always get asked from people on radio, television or live in person is: *At what age should we turn these over to our kids?* I always reply *"As soon as possible!"*

Thinking from "Reaction" to RETHINKING

WHY YOUR ATTITUDE MUST CHANGE, how to do it, and what you will get when you do.

"Men are disturbed not by things, but by the views which they take of them."
Epictetus - Stoic philosopher from first century A.D.

Life is 10 percent what really happens to you and 90 percent how you choose to rethink. In this chapter, I want you to learn how to step back and begin to rethink all situations you come in contact with as a parent. I want you to begin recognizing that 98 percent of the situations you and your kids will deal with won't kill you or them! They'll frustrate you, but won't kill any of you.

In 98 percent of these situations we come upon, we can "choose" to step back and rethink the situation. I believe that only two percent of the time do we as parents need to step in and "react" to the situation at hand. This is when your sons or daughters are at risk of either hurting themselves or hurting others. Stepping in and taking control over your child's behavior is the right thing to do here.

Choosing to think the way we want

Research indicates that over 12,000 thoughts enter our brain each day. Now that's a lot of information! If you can accept responsibility for how you choose to interpret these thoughts, then you have the opportunity to be more positive in your outlook toward yourself and others. As a result, you can teach and model to your children how to develop a positive view of life's daily events. **We must provide them with opportunities to accept responsibility for how they're choosing to think, act and feel, regarding life's**

daily events.

We're never innocent bystanders in life. We need to teach and model to our kids that life is a series of experiences in which we're always involved. As we're involved with our experiences, we have perceptions and evaluations, called thoughts, that form into beliefs and finally lead to **choices** in our behavior.

These beliefs about ourselves, others and the world around us are formed from the time we can begin to think, and are molded by our parents, teachers, friends, religious teachings, extended family members, and so on. When you really think about this, you'll begin to understand that we're not born prejudiced about anyone or anything; we become so through our experiences and teachings. That's why our role as parents in eradicating hatred and other forms of prejudice starts with the information we provide to our kids about events or people.

If our viewpoint is negative, it's likely our kids' viewpoints will be negative. One of the most important lessons, then, for children to learn is to take total personal responsibility for their inner life, their thinking, and, as a result, their actions and their feelings. As parents, we can start by understanding that problems with people or events begin with how we choose to think about those people or events. And we have total control over how we choose to think in these situations.

On the other hand, most people think the **CAUSE** of their problems is something "out there." They think other people, situations or things **CAUSE** them stress, frustration, pain and problems. **Thinking this way directs most people to act in an attempt to change or manipulate "out there"** to get what they want in order to feel good.

You can see their focus isn't on how they're choosing to think. It's focused on "out there" and that's a setup for frustration. If "out there" doesn't change enough, most people feel bad. Either way, many people allow "out there" to have enormous power over how they think, act and feel. Thinking this way will result in them "reacting" to the world around them.

An important step in the productive thinking strategy to save your sanity is to **step back and rethink what problems really are.** This is totally opposite of reacting and looking to "out there" as the cause of your problems. When you have a problem, it's because you're experiencing a **DIFFERENCE** between what you want and what you have. **It's the difference, NOT THE ENVIRONMENT,** that causes the negative feelings.

Think of a child who has a messy room. As the parent, you want a clean room, but what you might have is a room where you can't even tell what color the carpet is! There's a definite difference between what you want and what you have. Are your initial thoughts negative? Perhaps they're something like, *"Johnny will never learn to clean up his room." "I get so frustrated with Susie."* or *"Jamie is such a pig."*

What actions do you think will result from generating those thoughts?

Will you be more apt to attempt to control them by yelling at them, screaming at them, criticizing them? Will you be more apt to threaten them with physical harm or with grounding just to get them to shape up? It's important for you to realize that your thoughts and actions will be like these, if you choose to "react" to the situation.

Take a look at some examples of the "want-have" differences some parents tell me about, and see if you can relate to any of them.

What parents HAVE	What parents WANT
• A child who's upset with them.	• A child who loves them.
• A child who talks back.	• A child who listens.
• A child who's disruptive.	• A child who minds.
• A child who's disrespectful.	• A respectful child.
• An alcohol/drug-using child.	• An alcohol/drug-free child.
• An irresponsible child.	• A responsible child.
• A child blaming others.	• A child having self-control.
• A child getting poor grades.	• A child on the honor role.
• A child in trouble with the law.	• A law-abiding child.
• An unmarried pregnant daughter.	• A pregnant married daughter.
• A messy bedroom.	• A clean bedroom.
• A child who's late for curfew.	• A child on time for curfew.
• A child who neglects chores	• A child who does chores.

These aren't unusual wants for a parent to have. Can you relate to having any of them? If so, you'll be able to compare the difference between what you want with what you have. The problem isn't in what parents want; it's whether the want is under our control or not.

Most of the wants listed above are admirable, but not always achievable. As you can see, what a parent actually has is often opposite. When that occurs, we feel FRUSTRATED. When we're frustrated, we must choose to think or act in some way to get what we want. This is where I want you to begin to accept frustration as a part of life, and **step back and rethink** about the problem at hand.

The problem is that we're not taught to think or act in efficient ways to close down the differences. I believe we've learned from our parents and from others around us to try to control what we can't control. We experience a problem and we want a solution to that problem, not tomorrow, right now! As a result, we generate "reacting" thoughts, actions and feelings. Unfortunately, when we're frustrated, we choose some pretty miserable options.

Frustration levels are like shirt sizes

Based on years of working with people, I believe the differences we experience can be like shirt sizes—small, medium, large or extra-large. **The size of the difference or problem you experience depends on how much "you" want what you want.** It isn't based on "out there" (other people, things or situations) and what they are or aren't doing.

One person will experience a traffic jam and react calmly, while another explodes with anger and frustration. One parent deals with frustrations calmly and directly, while another turns red, foams at the mouth, swears, screams, yells and threatens. They respond or "react" differently because one of them knows he has almost no control over external circumstances but total control over himself, while the other assumes and believes exactly the opposite.

Same frustration, different responses

Reacting Parents

See a problem, feel frustrated and want immediate changes to occur.

Think, *"How can I change my child to get what I want?"*

Try to get "out there" to change by using manipulation, threats, coercion, rules, and consequences or punishment.

When these choices work, they feel reinforced and powerful, and attribute their success to their power over their children. When these attempts to gain control don't work—that is, when "out there" doesn't change—most people become more frustrated and try even harder to manipulate the situation by:
- Threatening physical harm.
- Psychological intimidation.
- Increasing negative consequences.

Rethinking Parents

See a problem, experience frustration, and step back and rethink the situation.

Think, *"What can I teach and model to my child that might influence him?"*

Focus on what they have control, influence and no control over in this situation.

Focus on giving the power, control and choices as well as the ownership of the problem over to their kids as quickly as possible. They understand that trying to change "out there" will result in even more frustration.

Teach and model that they have the power, control and choices, as well as the responsibility, to deal with the decisions they're making in their own problem situations. Teach and model that Rethinking provides you with power in life.

- Emphasizing rules that "must" be obeyed or else.
- Offering rewards as incentives.
- Bribing with money or material possessions.
- Excessively yelling, screaming, threatening and other powering behaviors.

Teach and model that Rethinking provides you with control.

Teach and model that Rethinking provides you with new choices.

Our perceptions control our thoughts, actions and feelings

The familiar cartoon of people looking at a glass of water provides the backdrop for some of our discussion regarding how thoughts direct actions. Our thoughts will influence whether we "react" or rethink about the problems we face each and every day as a parent. It's not "out there," or the situation, that creates our choice of what we do or don't do in any situation. I want you to learn that it's our thoughts that will determine if we're going to "react" to problems that arise, or if we'll step back and rethink those problems.

When you think about the example in the above drawing, it's the same glass of water everyone's looking at, yet some perceive it as half-full, and others as half-empty.

The glass is the same size, the **interpretations** are different. It's how we "choose to think" about the situation that's the problem. Some people have developed a pattern of thinking that allows them to look at the same situation, but in a more productive way. They've trained their brain to rethink, not react. You can too.

I want you to rethink with me that your brain is dual purpose; it's your best friend and also your worst enemy. The difference is in how you choose to think about certain situations that come up in life. You need to train your brain to rethink about situations and not react to them. Hopefully, you can see that by simply using *The Six Critical Questions* we've learned so far, we can train our brains to think differently about the daily problems of living.

You may have heard the saying that no two people have ever read the same book. You might ask several people the same question regarding the book, *"What was the author saying in the story?"* Each person might view the story differently. People's interpretation of a situation can be as unique as their fingerprints.

One person's perception may be close to or tremendously different than another's, which makes our role as parents interesting. We think a situation occurred one way and our kids see it in a different way.

How many times have we as parents heard something from our kids and reacted to what we've heard without gathering all the facts? A person who rethinks is open to the possibility that a situation may have many interpretations. Thus, a rethinker steps back and evaluates situations before acting. A rethinker asks lots of questions about a situation before formulating any opinions. This is something we need to train our brains to do.

As an example, there's a story of a man driving along a country road in his brand new car, enjoying not only the car, but also the drive and the scenery. Suddenly, a child stepped from the brush and threw a stone at his car.

The man stopped the car, backed up in anger and disgust, and, as you can imagine, was "madder than could be" at this kid. He began to give it to him with both barrels, when the boy interrupted: *"I'm sorry about throwing the stone at your car, but I didn't know any other way to get you to stop. It's my brother; he's in the ditch and he's hurt very bad."*

Would your interpretation of the situation change? Would you still be "madder than could be?" Would you choose to use different words with the child as a result?

In many of my talks around the world, I use a slide that depicts a father and son at the breakfast table. The son is chomping away at his cereal, while Dad is reading the paper. The caption above the Dad reads, *"What's this about a serious drug problem at your school?"* while the son responds, *"Golly no, Dad, you can get all you want!"*

This cartoon points out the fact that even with only verbal information, two people can have different interpretations. I'd love to guess what the next cartoon might be. If the father perceives the son's comment in a negative way, he'll probably react and say things like, *"I better never catch you using drugs!"* followed by a lengthy lecture or sermon on the evils of drugs, the types of people that use drugs, what happens to people when they use drugs, and so on.

On the other hand, if the father chooses to step back and rethink this situation in a neutral way, he'll act in a neutral way. Most likely, he'll choose to ask questions in a calm, information-getting fashion, rather than an accusatory way. You can see that in a simple situation like this the father can think about the event in many different ways, or he can choose to step back and RETHINK the situation by asking more questions about his son's statement. By stepping back and rethinking, the father can start by ALLOWING his son to clarify his statement in order to gain a better and more accurate interpretation of the event.

How we interpret events around us

From the examples provided so far, you can clearly see that your feelings result entirely from the way you interpret events. Your anger, sadness, depression, loneliness, calmness, love, joy or other feelings are directed by **how you choose to perceive an event.**

Of course, your thoughts, your feelings and your actions are **influenced** by external events, such as the weather, your kids, your spouse, and your job, to name just a few. Your physical make-up, intellectual ability, health, handicapping conditions, past experiences in your childhood, last week, and yesterday, also influence these thoughts, feelings and actions.

Notice I chose to use the word **influence** rather than control. If we truly believe that external events direct our behaviors, then we'd be acting essentially like machines that have no ability to choose. I want you to teach and model that we have the Power of Choice.

We all know people who continue to express feelings about something that happened quite some time ago. They continue to talk about the "raw deal" they got from their old boss, about their spouse who separated or divorced them, about their father or mother who left them, or about the death of a loved one.

Sure, these situations will influence people. But doesn't it get a little old, listening to them expressing these feelings over and over? What are the potential prices or consequences these people will pay for choosing to stay at just a feeling level? Are others likely to move toward them, or away from them, when they're like this? Will expressing their feelings move them closer to solving their problems?

As I've already stated, our interpretations direct our actions and our subsequent feelings. Not all feelings are positive, of course, and it is appropriate and necessary to express feelings like sadness, depression, anger or hurt. The loss of a friend, the death of a loved one, the loss of a job, the yelling match with a child, leave most people with intense feelings.

To express your feelings is to be human. How we express them varies from person to person. Losing a spouse will generate a wealth of emotion. Losing a job may do the same. **The key question is: how long are you going to continue to talk about, display, or express these feelings about**

an event that has already happened? In other words, how long are you going to complain, whine, and be angry, miserable and depressed about something you have either no control over or at best just influence over?

These are very powerful questions we need to ask ourselves in order to go beyond where most people are today. We need to teach and model these questions to our kids, so they can become as strong as we're becoming.

Another key point here is that we as parents need to teach and model to our kids that we may not be in control of the events around us, but are in control of how we interpret them. This is what I call rethinking. And beyond just rethinking these events, we need to teach and model that we have complete control over how we continue to think, act or feel about events in our lives.

Evaluating our present thoughts, actions and feelings

The first step in taking more effective control in your life as a parent is to step back, rethink and begin to evaluate your own thoughts, actions and feelings. Hopefully, you'll be able to ask yourself personal value judgment questions about your present parenting, such as, *"Is how I choose to think about my children right now affecting how I deal with them?" "Are thinking these thoughts going to help me?" "Is what I'm presently doing to solve my problems with my kids helping me develop responsible, healthy kids?" "Am I an effective model to my kids of staying calm in a problem situation?"*

It's important for us to understand that change doesn't take place in our own parenting style until we realize that what we're currently thinking and/or doing isn't working well enough. Challenging your present thinking about yourself and the world around you is a big step. It goes beyond where most people are, but that's what I want you to do.

Most people evaluate others and the outside world first, not themselves. Unfortunately, this sets up a "reaction" approach to the problem at hand. Honestly answering the value judgment questions above will create the necessary motivation to look for better choices, in order to narrow those differences between what we now have as a parent and what we want.

KEY POINTS TO REMEMBER

- Ninety-eight per-cent of all problems experienced in our lives or our kids' lives may frustrate us or them, but won't kill any of us.
- Ten percent of life is what really happens to you and 90 percent is how you choose to either react or rethink.
- It's not "out there" that creates our choice of what we do or not do in any situation. It's our interpretation of "out there," followed by the choices we make.
- Our interpretations of events need to be challenged for evidence of their

accuracy.

- The first step in taking more effective control in your life as a parent is to step back, rethink and begin to evaluate your own thoughts, actions and feelings.
- Problems are simply differences between what you want and what you have.
- Our thoughts direct our actions and our feelings.
- Our thoughts, actions, and feelings can be chosen as positive, negative or neutral—it's our choice.
- Our degree of frustration is directly related to how much we want what we want.
- The messages we provide to our children will influence their self-talk statements in either a positive or negative way.

AREAS TO PRACTICE AND SHARE

Ask yourself two questions:
1. Am I doing this now?   2. Am I going to start doing this?

- Make an effort to help your kids identify how they're choosing to set themselves up for frustration by what they think, say or do regarding an event they've experienced.
- Make a commitment to challenge and debate your own negative thinking patterns by asking the questions *"How is choosing to think this way helping me?"* or *"Will continuing to think this way help me solve this problem or keep this a problem?"*
- As a reminder to what a problem really is, tape the word **difference** to the bathroom mirror, refrigerator door, the dashboard of your car, in your workplace, or any other place where you spend time.
- Make a plan to help your kids observe people around them and try to identify the "difference" people are having when they're frustrated. You can have some fun figuring out what they "want" and what they "have."
- Once you've identified their "wants" and "haves," have your kids decide which wants are under a person's control, influence or no control.
- Talk to and teach your children that **problems are a part of life.** The key to solving problems begins in how a person chooses to think about those problems.
- Help your kids see the "poor choices" people might make in their attempts to get what they want. Talk with them about the consequences suffered when making these poor choices.
- Sit down with your kids and identify people in the world who are negative in their thoughts and their actions. Brainstorm with them how choosing to be this way affects various aspects of their lives

Typical Problems...Dr. Mike's Practical Solutions

Insert the problem here.

WHO owns the
PROBLEM?

WHO owns the
RESPONSIBILITY?

WHO made the
DECISIONS?

WHO has the
POWER?

WHO has the
CONTROL?

WHO makes the
CHOICES?

CHARACTER

©Michael M. Thomson Ph.D. 1995

Pre-School/Elementary School

Typical Problem:

"My children know when to act like brats whenever we're in a public place, like a mall or a restaurant. They seem to believe they can get what they want out of us any time they want. They really know how to push our buttons. What can I do to not lose my cool?"

Practical Solution:

Don't think for a minute that our kids are dummies. They know exactly what they're doing when they act up in public places. They know the last thing parents want is to create a scene in public. You can see how easy it would be to "react" and give in to their demands. Don't give in or give up. Rethink. This is the time for the "helmet and flak jacket."

Your children have the power, control and the choice to act the way they want to anywhere they want to. I recommend you do a couple of things here. Walk away if you need to. If the behavior continues to the point of disrupting other people, then I suggest you step in.

If they turn the volume up on their unruly behavior, don't give in. Simply turn around and head back to the car or to an unpopulated area of the place you're in and do what you'd have done if you were at home. If they choose not to pull it together, you need to be prepared to leave the area and return home. As frustrating as this may be for you or others with you, the message needs to be delivered to your children that their behavior is the reason you left the area and/or went home.

I suggest children suffer some additional consequences for their poor-choice behavior when they get home. This could be not playing with their special toys, not watching television, not going out to play, etc. Explain that you're not "taking" these things away from them; their poor choices are. They're being removed because they were the ones not making the good choices at the restaurant, at the mall, etc.

When planning to go to these areas again, you need to issue stern warnings to your children *before* you go, as a reminder of what you expect from them. Obviously, I also want you to make sure that you "catch 'em being good," when they are making the right choices.

Middle School

Typical Problem:

"My child has a tough time getting his school work done. We try to get him to sit down and focus on it at the dining room table. What happens is he spends a lot of time scribbling, watching television, listening to his stereo with his headphones on, and getting up and walking around aimlessly. What should I do?"

Practical Solution:

One thing is for sure: you'll never turn this type of child into a scholar by nagging, threatening, pushing or punishing. These choices will only lead to creating one more problem on top of what you're trying to solve. Focus on what you have control over here, which is yourself. Sit down with your child and discuss the issue. Reach an agreement with him, and his teacher if need be, about what grade he should be able to attain. Don't set it too high or too low. Make it within his reach. Question whether it's a problem of laziness, or of ability?

If you believe it's due to laziness on your child's part, you may want to consider withholding the privileges he seems more interested in until he completes his assigned schoolwork. You need to put on the helmet and flak jacket. As a parent, you have the authority to grant or withhold privileges. If you see a change in behavior, you can begin to give back those lost privileges.

On the other hand, you might find that your child doesn't have the ability to meet your expectations. You need to step back and rethink that your child might be the type of person who isn't going to be a wizard in the academic world. Remember to not attempt to force or squeeze him into the mold you want for him. Teachers and school counselors can help you find more reasonable expectations. Make your child feel the sky's the limit, but remember, not everyone can be a rocket scientist.

High School

Typical Problem:

"I was notified by the secretary of the mall security office that my child and her friends were being detained in the security office. They were all brought down by store officials for shoplifting. They want me to come down and pick up my child. This is so embarrassing. What should I do?"

Practical Solution:

Step back and rethink the problem here. Approach the situation with the idea that you want more information on what actually happened. Ask the security staff to help you out. If you find out that your child owns the problem, then acknowledge this and inquire what the consequences will be for her poor choices. Support the security staff for their input and recommendation in dealing with this matter.

On the other hand, if you find your child wasn't shoplifting and didn't know it was going on, but was with the group that was, this takes on a different meaning. Your child knows that regardless of what other people do, she does have control over her choices. You need to let her know this and "catch her being good," for making these choices.

However, you might find out that she knew in advance that her friends were in fact shoplifting. In that case, the situation takes on yet a different meaning. Your child needs to know that, as soon as she became aware of her friends' intentions, and actions, she needed to either say something to them to try and stop them, or walk away.

Moral courage, integrity and character require effort to do the right thing. Her friends may get mad at her, or drop her as a friend, but teach her this is the price you sometimes pay for doing the right thing. But it's a price worth paying in the long run.

Rethinking from "Problems" to OPPORTUNITIES

MASTERING THE STRATEGY of turning all problems into opportunities. Unlocking your potential.

How times have changed

Two caterpillars were crawling along the ground when a butterfly flew over them. As they looked up, one nudged the other and said: "You couldn't get me up in one of those things for a million dollars."

How like that caterpillar so many folks are: wrapped in little cocoons, inching along the ground, resisting change, fearing change, even a change that will transform them into something beautiful and set them free to fly.

In our lifetime, we've experienced enormous changes! But that's nothing new. Poets and philosophers, preachers and authors have talked about change since the dawn of history. More than 2,500 years ago, the Greek philosopher Heraclitus declared: "Nothing endures but change." And 19th century American preacher and orator Henry Ward Beecher proclaimed: "Our days are a kaleidoscope. Every instant a change takes place."

Some of the changes we've seen have been for the better, while others have created problems. And with those problems came a need for a change in thinking—one that views "problems" as opportunities.

The late Eric Hoffer, American author and social philosopher, once said: "In times of change learners inherit the earth, while the learned find themselves beautifully equipped to deal with a world that no longer exists." I see that as a challenge to avoid the trap of the status quo and to continue learning from every one of our experiences in life.

Accept that the past is the past. Don't disregard it, but learn from it. Choose to view life as a series of problems that can be turned into learning opportunities. One of the most unfortunate lessons a child can learn in his journey through life is to give up and say, *"I can't do it!" "It's too hard." "What if I fail?"* We need to teach and model the opposite to them.

Problems are opportunities in disguise

I want you to rethink that all problems are really opportunities in disguise. Having problems in your life isn't the end of the world. With this in mind, there are three themes I want to teach you so you can teach and model them to your kids.

1. The first theme, which we've already discussed, is that: **"The only people without problems are dead."** Your kids will experience problems. They'll fight with their brothers or sisters, get in disagreements with their parents, have difficulty in school, get cut from the team, get in a funk about something, and so on. That's life. The difference between the person who chooses to stay stuck with a problem and another who views a problem as an opportunity in disguise lies in the way they choose to think. And what we're learning here is choosing to step back and rethink all problems.

2. The second theme is: **"The world is filled with jerks."** Some of you have dated them, married them or worked "for" them. Your kids will meet some jerks, in the form of friends, girlfriends, boyfriends, teachers, coaches, and maybe even parents. That's just life.

    What makes the difference is that a rethinker chooses to *learn* from jerks. By that, I don't mean following their example—quite the contrary! They always teach us how not to think, act and feel. If you want to be a great parent, look for jerk parents; watch them, listen to them, do the complete opposite—and you'll be a great parent!

3. The third theme is: **"In a tornado, even a turkey can fly!"** I don't want you to ever give up. I want you to teach and model to your kids to never give up when problems arise. You both need to understand that even in tough times (tornadoes) you can make the right choice.

    Parents who go through a divorce (definite tornado for both parents and kids) can teach and model that they will get through this, learn from it, and make it an opportunity for growth. Successful parents are always searching for ways to improve, grow and strengthen themselves and their kids. Success begets success.

Productive parents choose to teach and model to their kids that the world is a smorgasbord of choices they have total control over. Productive parents teach and model that problems encountered in life become opportunities to learn.

Productive parents teach and model to their kids that they have the power and the control to rethink and make the right choices in life, even when no one's watching. After all, this is the true test of a person of good character. And being a person of good character is what parents want for their kids.

Take Walt Disney, for example. He went around asking people to invest in a theme park idea of his and was turned down 302 times! Colonel Sanders was turned down more than a thousand times on a chicken idea he had! Edison failed over 10,000 times in developing the light bulb! But when interviewed about these "failures," Edison summed it up perfectly by saying: "They were not failures, they were learning opportunities."

How many times do we as parents give up when trying to solve frustrating problems? How many times do our kids do the same thing? The key for us as parents is that we need to influence our kids to stick with it when problems arise. We need to teach and model for our kids that Disney, Sanders and Edison never gave up. They were truly examples of believing you're never stuck unless you *choose* to think, act or feel stuck.

It takes effort to turn problems into opportunities. I think Disney, Edison, and Sanders would agree with me on this. But once you obtain the courage to start moving forward into thinking productively that problems can be opportunities, life will begin to change for you, and for others around you. You can teach and model this to your kids in all situations.

Parents must recognize that to have effective change, their kids must change, and for their kids to change, their thinking must change. Parents are the ones who provide this climate of change. They encourage risk taking.

People who react and focus on "problems" will:
- Think stress is something to be avoided.
- Believe that "out there" controls their thoughts, actions and feelings.
- Think, act and feel out of control when stress arises.
- Give to others with the intent of getting something in return.
- Think of self first, before others.
- Think winning or being on top is the only goal.
- Meet their needs "through" others.
- Blame "out there" for their frustrations.
- Look at life as a series of outcomes to be conquered.
- Focus on getting what they want when they want it.
- Think and act in the areas of "no control" most of the time.

People who choose to step back, rethink and view problems as "opportunities" will:

- Rethink that stress, the difference between what they have and what they want, isn't always to be feared; it can be an opportunity for growth.
- Understand that they control only themselves and the choices they make.
- Look for situations that can be turned into opportunities to practice *The Eight Areas of The Power of Productive Choices* and *The Six Critical Questions.*
- Step back and take a "camera check" of the problem at hand. This allows them the opportunity to look at the problem from various angles, asking questions such as, "What might others say the problem is here?"
- Identify what choices have been working and not working to solve the problem at hand.
- Ask others for their input in solving the problem at hand.
- Discover that their thinking about a problem directs their actions and their feelings. They can choose how they want to think.
- Discover that what they can control, what they can influence, and what they have no control over in problem situations frees them from the degree of frustration they're experiencing.
- Give up the notion that they're forced to think, act or feel a certain way, and take control of choosing to think, act and feel the way they want to.
- Rethink that all behaviors are purposeful to meet one or more of their internal psychological needs. Disrupting or disruptive behaviors will be viewed as red flags, indicating frustrated need areas.
- Rethink and enjoy life as a series of process steps toward an open outcome.
- Observe the choices others make when they're frustrated.
- From these observations, you can learn new choices for dealing with similar situations in the future.
- Believe that giving to others is for the sake of giving just to give and not to get something in return.

Using problems as opportunities for growth

If you go outside in the dead of winter in a short sleeve shirt and shorts, you'll probably end up catching a cold. If you cut yourself with a knife, you'll bleed. If you drink too much alcohol, you'll become impaired.

Most of us will agree that these are the natural consequences of the poor choices a person makes in these situations. I think we'd all agree that we could turn these situations into learning opportunities if we step back, rethink and evaluate the choices made at the time. Hopefully, we're smart enough to make better choices the next time these same situations occur.

Let's take a look at the following problems kids can present to us:
- Forgetting their lunch.
- Forgetting their homework.
- Forgetting to set their alarm.
- Getting a speeding ticket.
- Drinking under age.
- Getting fired from a job.
- Not coming home on time.
- Getting in trouble at school.

In each of these problem situations, I think you can see how easy it might be as a parent to "react" and focus on the "problem" at hand. You could easily picture a parent saying: *"How could you forget your lunch, forget to do your homework, forget to set your alarm, get a speeding ticket, drink at your age, get fired from your job, not come home on time, or get in trouble at school? What were you thinking?"*

You can easily see how a parent's tone of voice, and perhaps some actions, could be out of control if these problems came up. Don't let this happen! Go back to what we've already studied and understand that your tone of voice is related to *you* choosing to *react* to the problem at hand.

Don't *react* to any of these problems anymore! There's a better strategy—a strategy to save your sanity. I want you to step back, rethink and focus on the problem at hand as an opportunity. It's an opportunity for you to teach and model to your kids how to use *The Eight Areas of The Power of Productive Choices* and *The Six Critical Questions* to rethink each of the problems they experience in life. For the sake of clarity, let's review the eight areas and tie them into the above examples:

1. Begin by changing your thinking from "reaction" to **RETHINKING.** As stated earlier, we have a choice to *react* to any of the above problems, many of which are generally not life threatening. The exceptions, of course, would include such poor choices as drinking and speeding, which are not only illegal, but can often lead to injury and death. In such situations, as we'll see later in this chapter, immediate parental action may be needed. However, in most cases, thinking clearly about the problem and not *reacting* to it is the key.

2. Start rethinking from "problems" to **OPPORTUNITIES.** Obviously, this is what this chapter's all about. Every one of the problems listed above can be viewed as a smorgasbord of choices kids made at the time. These

poor choices don't make them "bad" kids. They're just poor choices that can be learned from and turned into opportunities for growth.

3. Next, rethink from "out of control" to **CONTROL.** You can take every problem listed above and help your kids step back, rethink, and separate each one into those they have control over, influence over, and no control over. Doing this with your kids will help them let go of problems they have no control or influence over, and get them focused, from this point forward, on what they have one hundred percent control over.

4. Begin rethinking from "no choice" to **CHOICE.** Once you've accepted that you have little or no control over the problems described above, you can focus on the choices you have one hundred percent control over.

5. Change your thinking from "controlling" to **RELATIONSHIP.** Because you're already stepping back, rethinking and using the previous four steps, your relationship with your child will be significantly different. You won't be reacting, focused on the problems, out of control with your emotions, out of control with your choices and perceived as controlling by your child.

   Your children will perceive you differently when you're trying to help them step back and rethink their problems. You're not placing blame on anything or anyone. You're just turning this problem into a learning opportunity. From this perception comes a relationship that's worth gold.

6. Begin rethinking from "wants" to **NEEDS.** In the list of problems above, you can teach and model to your kids that they may not be able to get what they want at the time, because of their poor choices, but that they can meet their needs in the long run. Because you're teaching your kids that they're never ever stuck unless they choose to think, act or feel stuck, you can teach them to brainstorm alternative choices that are available to help them solve their existing problem. By doing this, you're teaching and modeling to them that their "wants" may be blocked at times but that they still have numerous options available to meet their needs.

7. Rethink from "external" to **INTERNAL.** The problems we listed above don't have anything to do with something "out there." The ownership of the problem rests with the child and the poor choices made at the time. Because you're teaching and modeling this strategy to your children, they'll begin to understand that they're not innocent bystanders in life. They have the internal power, control and choices to rethink all problems they encounter.

8. In your rethinking, switch from "outcome" to **PROCESS.** The problems listed above may not be solved right away. In fact, some may create additional problems for your kids. Teach and model to them that the solutions will take time and patience on their part. Each "baby step" choice they make in using the strategy outlined here will be one step beyond where most people are today when dealing with problems.

Now that we've reviewed *The Eight Areas of The Power of Productive Choices* in rethinking problems, let's work our way through *The Six Critical Questions.*

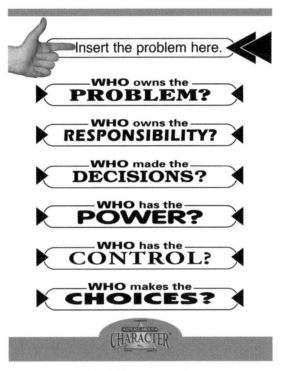

1. **"Who Owns the Problem?"** Look at the list of problems.
   The child owns each and every one of them. Period, end of sentence.

2. **"Who Owns the Responsibility?"** Again, the child is responsible for every one of them.

3. **"Who Made the Decisions?"** It's critical for us to recognize that, in each of these problems, the child, and no one else, decided to make the poor choice.

4. **"Who Has the Power?"** I hope you can immediately see that the kids had the internal power of choice in each of these problem situations.

5. **"Who Has the Control?"** Unless your child has some out-of-control biochemical disorder, he or she has control over the choices made in each of these problem areas.

6. **"Who Makes the Choices?"** You know I'm going to say that in each of these problem situations the child decides to make either a good choice or a poor choice

Earlier I stated that 98 percent of the problem situations in life won't kill us. Frustrate us, yes; kill us, no. In two percent of life's problem situations, we need to react; we need to step in and take control over our child's choices and a problem situation. Here are the areas where I think we need to step in and take control:

• If a person's in physical jeopardy. For example: a suicide attempt or threat; a child inflicting harm on himself or herself; a child running into oncoming traffic; arrests for speeding and reckless driving; or someone abusing alcohol or other drugs.
• When a child's in jeopardy of hurting another person. For example: someone who's threatening another person either physically or psychologically, or using anything that could induce or inflict harm on another person.
• When a child's in jeopardy of damaging property. This includes angry, temper-tantrum outbursts. For example: one young man I worked with attempted to remodel his parents' house with a hockey stick by breaking everything in sight. (This is the time to dial 911 and let the kid sit in the "Cross Bar Hilton" for the night.) Rethinking the problem can wait till the next day when the storm clouds have dissipated.
• When the child's health is in jeopardy. For example: refusing to eat, refusing to get appropriate vaccinations, or refusing medical attention when needed.
• When a child's too young to understand. For example: a child under the age of four shouldn't be expected to be responsible all the time. We can't expect them to be miniature adults, because they've had very little experience with responsibility.

KEY POINTS TO REMEMBER

• The only people without problems are dead.
• The world is filled with jerks.
• In a tornado, even a turkey can fly!

- Accept that the past is the past. Don't disregard it, learn from it. Choose to view life as a series of problems that can be turned into learning opportunities.
- All "problems" are really opportunities in disguise.
- Teach and model that the world is a smorgasbord of choices you have total control over.
- You're never stuck unless "you choose" to think, act or feel stuck.
- Ninety-eight percent of all problems experienced in our lives or our kids' lives may frustrate us, but won't kill us.
- We can choose to step back and rethink in 98 percent of the problem situations in life.
- In two percent of life's situations, we need to react by stepping in and taking control.

AREAS TO PRACTICE AND SHARE

Ask yourself two questions:
1. Am I doing this now?   2. Am I going to start doing this?

- The minute a problem comes up, help your child rethink and not react by keeping your tone of voice calm. This will take practice on your part, but it will set the tone for rethinking a problem situation.
- If your child's frustration was the result of another person's poor choices; help your child step back and rethink the situation, and look at the other person's choices as a learning experience about - "how not to be" in life.
- Grab every opportunity to teach your child that problem situations you see on television, read about in the news, or observe in life can be solved through rethinking and not reacting.
- On the flip side, grab every opportunity to teach your child how people can choose to *react* to problem situations and keep themselves out of control for as long as they choose.
- Keep the *"Who Owns the Problem?"* poster prominently displayed where your kids can see it. Use it as a reference tool to solve problems more effectively.

Typical Problems...Dr. Mike's Practical Solutions

Insert the problem here.

► **WHO** owns the **PROBLEM?** ◄

► **WHO** owns the **RESPONSIBILITY?** ◄

► **WHO** made the **DECISIONS?** ◄

► **WHO** has the **POWER?** ◄

► **WHO** has the **CONTROL?** ◄

► **WHO** makes the **CHOICES?** ◄

IT'S ALL ABOUT **CHARACTER** INC.

©Michael M. Thomson Ph.D. 1995

Pre-School/Elementary

Typical Problem:

"I fight with my kids to get them out of bed and I fight to get them into bed. I talk and talk and they never listen to me. You take a privilege away and they say 'so,' or 'doesn't bother me,' or the classic 'whatever.' My kids tell me 'you're not the boss of me' on a regular basis. This is nuts! I'm counting the days until they're 18! I feel like I'm losing my mind. I can't stand it anymore."

Practical Solution:

Okay, settle down. Step back, relax and "take a chill pill," as they say. Choose to rethink that "this too shall pass." You say you can't stand it. Well you are standing it. I know you don't like it at the time, but this is what parenthood's all about. It's not all giggles. There will be times when you feel like this—and your feelings are legitimate.

But once you recognize you're feeling like this, don't stay at the feelings level and lament about those feelings for long. You need to step back, rethink, and focus your energy on turning this into an opportunity. It's an opportunity for you to throw the flag on the field and call timeout.

Getting up and going to bed are the kids' problems, not yours. Turn the problems over to them. Let them know what you expect, and be willing to discuss your expectations with them. The bottom line is that once you've set the structure for getting up and going to bed, let your kids know the responsibility is theirs. If they choose to fight with you, then you choose not to fight. *"I do jokes, I do windows, I don't do arguments,"* will be your theme.

Rethink and focus on what you have total control over: the removal of privileges; taking them to special places; making special treats or meals; driving them places; or anything else where you have to lift a finger to help out. I'm suggesting you *calmly* let your kids see that, if they choose to behave in an out-of-control way, you're choosing to behave in a controlled way.

Will it take time to see changes? Maybe, maybe not. But that's not your problem, responsibility or decision. You're not the one with the power, control or choice to do anything about it. Your kids are.

Middle School

Typical Problem:

"My middle school daughter is always on the Internet. She's emailing her friends everyday. I happened to read a hard copy of one of her emails left on her dresser. It was from her boyfriend. It was so sexually graphic about what the two of them have been doing that I was sick. I was angry and appalled, but, if I have to admit to her that I was prying into her privacy, she'll never trust me again. What should I do?"

Practical Solution:

What should you do? You don't want to pry into a behavior like sex with your daughter for fear she'd get mad at you! C'mon, now's the time for you to put the flak jacket and helmet on and step in. Whether you found out "private" information about your daughter's behavior via her journal, a handwritten note, an overheard phone conversation, or the Internet, YOU have acquired the PROBLEM, RESPONSIBILITY and the DECISION to do something about it.

This is the bad behavior I've been talking about that you need to step in on. Getting pregnant, being used as a sex toy, or acquiring a sexually transmitted disease, should be enough to get you to take action.

Trusting a child doesn't mean abdicating responsibility. It's time for you to review the structure you expect from her in regard to dating, sex, and relationships in general. Just because a person has a penis or vagina doesn't mean that person is mature. She needs your help and guidance right now. Not tomorrow—now!

The other thing you need to drill into your head is that your kids are not "entitled" to privacy when their decisions or activities are going to either hurt themselves or others (the potential unborn child). Explain to her that you believe snooping through her backpack, dresser drawers, clothes, room or computer is destructive to an ongoing relationship between you.

HOWEVER, when something like this indicates her behavior is potentially going to hurt her or someone else, all bets are off on the privacy/trust issue. As a parent, you have a moral responsibility to act. You're stepping in on her *behavior* and it's the behavior you need to keep your focus on, not her as a person. Standing up against "evil behavior" brings out the difference between good and evil. Without taking a stand against this behavior, we're not part of the solution, but actually a part of the problem.

High School

Typical Problem:

"My son has a temper that would rival any tough kid you could think of. He's always swearing at me, telling me he hates me, threatening to run away, and throwing fits of anger that result in household possessions being damaged or destroyed on occasion. It starts when I get him up in the morning. He's in a bad mood because I don't have clean clothes for him to wear, don't have the right breakfast or packed lunch for him, and don't want to give him a ride to school. How am I going to make him behave and save what's left of my own sanity?"

Practical Solution:

Here's a classic example of *"Who Owns the Problem?"* The parent is taking on the problem, responsibility, decisions, power, control and choices here. You can just feel the tension as a result. But rethink with me about who's really responsible for setting up this tension.

You've got it, the parent. What needs to happen quickly is for the parent to take responsibility only for what he or she chooses to do, and turn over to that son what he has total control over doing. This deterioration in behavior on the child's part hasn't happened overnight; it has probably gone on for many years.

It might have started with the parent taking on the child's responsibility for going to bed and getting up on time, getting his own clothes and lunch ready, arranging for his own ride to and from school, getting his homework done, cleaning his room, and taking care of his own day-to-day attitude and responsibility for living in a place called home.

A *house* is where you check in, grab a towel, bar of soap, and check for messages at the front desk. A *home* is where you share in the responsibility of getting things done on a daily basis.

A house is where you'll hear: *"This is the last time I'll do this for you,"* on a regular basis. You may also hear it in a home, but the chances of hearing it over and over are slim and none.

Bottom line: stop taking on your kids' problems and responsibilities. Because you have high school age kids, trust me, they won't say to you: *"Wow, what a great idea, we should have done this years ago!"* You'll hear a tremendous amount of whining, anger, pouting, threatening, and downright nastiness.

It will start with the morning wakeup routine to being late for school and wanting you to lie to the person from school calling about them being late. You know they got up late because they either didn't set the alarm or turned it off. Just hand the phone to them and say, *"It's the school calling about why you're not there."*

If your child refuses to talk with the caller or doesn't tell the truth, it's up to you to inform the school that your child was at home without your permission. Let school officials know what you're doing in your attempt to get things to change and that you'll support them for taking the same stand in holding your children accountable for *their* poor choices.

Do not give in. Talk the talk and walk the walk. The ball is now in their court as to their choices from this point forward. If they attempt to destroy property, threaten you with bodily harm, or run away, you need to do what you have control over, which includes letting the authorities know of any threats and asking for their help and intervention if need be.

Drawing a "new line" in the sand won't be easy, after years of them walking over the line, but it is necessary. You will see change, not so much because they change, but because you've changed. And that *is* something you have control over.

Rethinking from "Out of Control" to CONTROL

3 SIMPLE CATEGORIES YOU MUST KEEP in your mind to save your sanity in parenthood.

In this chapter, we'll take a look at how productive people choose to step back, rethink and separate every one of their problem situations into three simple categories: what they have control over; what they have influence over; and what they have no control over.

Just doing this simple step whenever you have problems in life will be worth the price of this book. I really mean this! Separating all problems into these three categories will not only save your sanity but, when you teach your kids to do it when problems arise in their lives, you'll be helping to save their sanity as well. It's such a simple step, but it's one that isn't used enough.

For some reason, when you become a parent, you're expected, unfortunately, to be "in control" of your child at all times. What a setup for burnout! Who's fed us this diet for such a long time? And how come we didn't challenge this way of thinking? The reason, I believe, is that these are different times than when we grew up. Different times demand different skills.

If there's one word that summarizes the conflicts between parents and their kids, it's the word, **"Control."**

"You cannot talk to me like that."
"You'll do what I say or else."
"I insist that you look at me right now."
"You will answer me this instant."
"I'm the parent here and you will always do what I say."
"I don't have to take this from you."

"I'm not gonna let you run this house one more minute."
"1, 2…if I get to 3, that little butt of yours is going to shine!"

Any of these sound familiar? They're examples of parents trying to **gain control** of their kids' behaviors. They're examples of how we set ourselves up to be actually "out of control" by thinking wrong! That's right, thinking wrong! We as parents are the ones with the "out of control" problem here. Don't believe me? Answer one question: who really has the control here, the parents or the kids? C'mon, you know the answer.

It's a tug of war!

Why do we as parents think we want control? Simple, It's need fulfilling for us. Why do we want our kids to be responsible and make good decisions? Simple, it's for the exact same reason. We all really get hung up on the issue of control. Why? You guessed it, because being "in control" fulfills a need for us.

Here's the problem. **If you as a parent perceive your need fulfillment as coming from how your kids think, act, or feel, then you're the one who's trying to control situations where you have either no control or at best just some influence.** It's a setup for frustration for you.

For example, if you want your kids to be nice to you and they're not, then you may say to them, *"To heck with you!" "Why should I be nice to you when I don't get nice back?"* Here's the kicker. ***You* are the one responsible for actually setting yourself up for being frustrated. Not the kids. *You*!**

There's a difference between what you want and what you have. This is what motivates you to react. The problem is that when you react and focus on "out there" as the problem, then you're immediately into an "out of control" area. That sets you up for **Parent Burnout.**

Let's face it, some people try desperately to control the events in their lives. They try to control their golf swing, their brother, their sister, their mother, their father, their kids, the weather, the flow of traffic, and so on. Can you see what the problem is here? The problem is that *you* have very limited control over these things. Some parents want what they want when they want it. So do some kids. As a result, we have a constant tug-of-war over the issue of control. Who's going to win?

Start taking control as a parent by **evaluating** what it is you want. Look at your wants in the areas of control, influence and no control. Change your thinking from wanting your children to think, act or feel the way you want them to think, act or feel, which is out of your control.

Begin rethinking that you're going to influence your kids by:
- Demonstrating caring to them (even if they don't reciprocate);
- Asking them questions (even if they don't answer them);
- Providing them with alternative choices they can make (even if they choose not to make better choices);
- Allowing them the freedom to think, act, or feel the way they want to (even if they choose not to think, act or feel differently);
- Working on building a positive relationship with them (even if they show no interest in a relationship with you).

All these attempts are within your control, regardless of how your kids respond.

Three simple categories to save your sanity

As a parent I can choose to teach and model my kids:

WHAT I CAN CONTROL
- The feelings I choose to have.
- Giving a compliment.
- Giving a hug.
- Smiling and saying "Hi" first.
- What I think of my child, myself and others.
- What questions I ask.
- Demonstrating caring.
- My tone of voice.
- How I view situations, people or events.
- How positive my attitude is.
- How long I feel frustrated.
- Providing alternative choices to problem solving.
- Becoming a teacher and model of *"The Eight Areas of The Power of Productive Choices."*
- Becoming a teacher and model of *"The Six Critical Questions."*
- Making statements of my wants and my expectations.

- Modeling efficient thinking, acting and feeling skills.
- My own example of good character by making good choices even when no one is watching.

WHAT I CAN INFLUENCE
- My child making good decisions. (Even when no one's watching.)
- Building a better relationship with my child.
- The home environment I create.
- My child's attitude.
- My child's feelings.
- My child's choices.
- The sense of safety and security my child feels.
- My child acting responsibly.
- My child developing the thinking and acting skills of what good character really is.
- My child using *"The Eight Areas of The Power of Productive Choices."*
- My child using *"The Six Critical Questions."*

WHAT I CANNOT CONTROL
- My child's ultimate choices.
- The way my child ultimately chooses to think, act or feel.
- Other parents' decisions on how they raise their kids.
- Effects of heredity or genetics.
- Disease.
- Injury.
- The weather.
- The past.
- Living forever.

Three simple categories to teach your kids

As a parent I can choose to teach my kids:

WHAT THEY (AS KIDS) HAVE CONTROL OVER
- How they choose to think.
- How they choose to act.
- How they choose to feel.
- Doing or not doing what you as a parent or others say.
- Getting up on time.
- Going to bed on time.
- Getting good grades in school.
- Doing or not doing their homework.
- Having a positive or negative attitude.
- What they say to others.

- Their tone of voice.
- Who their friends are.
- The choices leading to losing or gaining privileges.
- Making good choices even when no one's watching (which is the definition of good character)
- Using *"The Eight Areas of The Power of Productive Choices."*
- Using *"The Six Critical Questions."*
- Demonstrating trust to you and others in their life.

WHAT THEY (AS KIDS) HAVE INFLUENCE OVER
- How you and others choose to think about, feel about or act toward them.
- Whether or not they choose to earn back lost privileges.
- Obtaining the grades they want.
- Their friends' decisions.
- Demonstrating trust to you and others.
- Demonstrating responsibility to you and others.
- Building and/or maintaining a relationship with someone in their life.

WHAT THEY (AS KIDS) HAVE NO CONTROL OVER
- The natural or logical consequences for their choices once they've been made.
- The way others choose to act, think or feel.
- The past choices they or others have made.
- Disease.
- Injury.
- Other parents' decisions on how they raise their kids.
- Effects of heredity or genetics.
- The weather.
- Living forever.

Share this list with your kids and see if they agree or disagree with it. They'll probably debate some of the items on the list. That's great! By debating these items, you'll have allowed them an opportunity to step back and rethink with you what you both have control over, influence over and no control over. This is a great way to open up dialogue about these three critical productive thinking areas.

It's also a great way for you to let your kids know you're not going to be a "controlling" parent, like some parents choose to be. You're modeling to them that you're focusing not only on teaching them but wanting them to take on the power, control and choices for their own lives. You'll be there to catch them making good choices, as well as to give them the heads-up when their choices are not so good.

If you, as a parent, make an effort to separate all the problem situations you encounter in life into the areas of control, influence and no control, you and your kids will find you have a tremendous amount of control in all your environments. You'll find you'll both worry less, become less anxious, angry, depressed and guilt-ridden. This becomes an incredible rethinking skill you can use for the rest of your life!

At best, you have influence

Below is a list of some issues that come up between parents and their kids. Read it and decide which ones *you* have control over, which ones *you* have influence over, and which ones *you* have no control over as a parent.

- Homework
- Swearing
- Temper tantrums
- Stealing
- Hair style
- Your kids' friends
- Saving money
- Feeling happy
- Who your kids marry

- Sexual activity
- Alcohol and other drug use
- Lying
- Dress style
- School attendance
- Getting a job
- Spending money
- Who your kids date
- Attitude (positive or negative)

As you can see, many of these are, at best, **areas we can influence.** You can have a lot of fun with this list. I believe that once you start rethinking about these areas in this way, you'll start to observe all problems and events you encounter in new and unexpected ways.

Whenever a topic comes up, you'll probably start to visualize these three categories in your head and begin to place the topic in the appropriate one. Hopefully, you'll begin to use these terms regularly, with your kids and with others in your life.

This strategy seems simple, but it's so powerful! You'll begin to notice others trying to control things they have no control over or, at best, just influence over. If you're like me, you'll see yourself in those "out of control" people and thank your lucky stars you aren't setting yourself up for that level of frustration!

Like everyone else, we as parents must let go of issues we have no control over, if we want to save our sanity. This doesn't mean we throw in the towel, but it does mean we become realistic about our own wants as parents, and with issues and problems presented to us in parenthood.

We need to understand and accept that we have no control over many wants, issues and problems in life, and may only be able to influence others. Our children may make choices that are the opposite of what we want. But as productive thinking parents, we know that, unless we put them under armed guard twenty-four hours a day, we can only influence, not control them, or the choices they ultimately make. Frustrating as it may be, that's reality.

BUT, don't forget the saying that *"evil will continue to triumph as long as good people choose to say and or do nothing."* Like me, you don't want evil to win. So speak up against it! When evil rears its ugly head, you need to say and or do something to intervene. Stand up for what's the right thing to say or do in a situation.

Let your kids know your opinion in these areas. Keep your helmet and flak jacket on, stand your ground regarding your beliefs, and reinforce them often. Of course, the forces of evil don't want you to speak out. But, as a parent who wants to build kids of good character, you know your job is to take on evil, get your feet wet, let the mud fly, and stand up and be noticed. This is influence at best!

Your job's not easy, but the reward for doing the right thing, even when it might be costly or risky, or when no one's watching, is the best payoff in the world. It's priceless. It's knowing your son or daughter is the kind of person you'd want for a son or daughter-in-law, your kid's coach or teacher, an employee of your company, or a leader in your community.

KEY POINTS TO REMEMBER

- You actually choose to set yourself up for frustration by choosing to think wrong.
- You need to separate all problems into areas where you have control, influence over, and no control over.
- With every problem your kids present to you, teach them to separate problems into what they have control, influence and no control over.
- Acknowledge that life is a series of problems to be solved.
- Accept that we have problems in life that we have either no control, or at best, just influence over.
- Allow your kids to take control over their own problems. By doing this, it will actually give you as a parent more control.
- Allow your kids to take on the responsibility for their own good and poor choices they make in life.
- Be willing to adjust your thinking and your actions in order to get what you want in your life. This is called compromising. Be willing to give a little in order to get a little. At the very least, it will lessen the degree of stress you experience.
- Understand that "evil will continue to triumph as long as good people choose to say and or do nothing." Be willing to step in front of evil behavior. Speak out against evil. Take a stand against it!
- Understand that you have control over four areas in any relationship: 1) demonstrating caring, 2) asking questions, 3) making statements and 4) providing alternative choices.

- Your tone of voice is critical in increasing your influence over other people. You're the only one who has control over raising or lowering it.
- Attempting to control how others think, act or feel will just create more problems for you. Remember that the more you attempt to control other people, the more out of control you become.
- Focusing on "out there" as the problem will create more "out of control" choices on your part. Your attempt to change "out there" will actually promote more frustration for you, not less. Instead, change your focus to what you have complete control over, which is how you choose to think, act and feel.

AREAS TO PRACTICE AND SHARE

Ask yourself two questions:
1. Am I doing this now?   2. Am I going to start doing this?

- Make a commitment to rethink all problems you encounter in terms of what you have control, influence and no control over. Teach and model this to your kids.
- Make an effort to work on using the words "control," "influence" and "no control" in your everyday language.
- When your kids are frustrated, look for opportunities to teach them to use these words.
- Identify areas where you and/or your kids may be seeking to control things, situations or people in which you either have no control over or just influence over.
- Let your kids know you want them to have power, control and choices at home, and elsewhere. Teach them that the responsibility for their good as well as their poor choices rests with the decisions they make.
- Look for opportunities in everyday life where you can teach your kids to speak out against evil situations and/or behavior.
- Look for opportunities for you and your kids to discuss movies and television sitcoms in how people are "choosing" to set themselves up for being "out of control" by thinking wrong. Applying the lessons in this chapter, discuss why you believe they're "out of control."
- Provide your kids the opportunity to take control over getting up and going to bed on time, taking showers or baths, cleaning their rooms, picking out their own clothes, picking up their own toys, taking care of the family pet, doing their own homework, and helping out around the home.
- Sit down with your kids and generate a list of typical problems you've both had in the past. Then figure out where you've both been attempting to control the things, people or situations to change, when in reality you had either just influence over or really no control over. Then discuss how

"controlling to always be in control" actually sets you up for more frustration.

- Use the following list and discuss what a person has control, influence or no control over:

sexual activity	violence
temper tantrums	crying
lying	choice of friends
dating	people liking you
pleasing people	getting others to do what you say
use of drugs	getting parents off your back
getting good grades	answering questions

- Sit down and discuss how, "You're never stuck unless you choose to think, act or feel stuck!" Discuss with them how words and phrases such as *"can't," "must," "have to," "I can't stand it," "I give up," "It will never work," "There's no way,"* keep you stuck in life. Brainstorm and generate a list of words and phrases a person can choose to think or say in order to get out of this type of "reactionary" thinking.
- Sit down and brainstorm about why excuses just keep a person stuck focusing on what either can't be done or shouldn't be done. Getting off *stuck* means making choices you have complete control over in solving the frustrations at hand.

Typical Problems…Dr. Mike's Practical Solutions

©Michael M. Thomson Ph.D. 1995

Pre-School/Elementary

Typical Problem:

"I keep yelling up the stairs to get my kids up for school. They don't get up and I'm going to be late for work. Finally, when they do get up, they yell at me, are in a bad mood and generally are a royal pain in the butt. What should I do?"

Practical Solution:

Let's get right to the use of *The Six Critical Questions* with this one. Who owns the problem, the responsibility and the decision of getting up or not getting up? The kids do. Who has the power, control and the choices in this situation? The kids! In the heat of the battle (you at the bottom of the stairs and your kids still in bed), you need to focus on what you have control over, which is your tone of voice, your caring, your questions and your statements.

My suggestion is that you calmly (even if you have to put a fist in your mouth) ask them to get up and get moving. Let them know, in a calm but stern voice, that you're going to be late for work and they're going to be late for school. If you need to go to the next level, because your kids haven't budged, calmly let them know that because they're "choosing" to stay in bed and be late, you'll be "choosing" to allow them to suffer the consequences, both at school and later on at home, for their poor choices.

The consequences at home could be anything from not being able to watch television, or go out with their friends, or play with a certain game or toy they like, not getting rides or money from you, or lowering their bedtime at night. Calmly explain that *you* won't be taking these things away from them, but that their poor choices will.

This is a very powerful statement to make to your kids. Don't argue with them—stick to your guns. As for school, let officials there know that, whatever the consequences for absence or lateness are, you support them.

On the other hand, *if* they get up promptly, catch them making the right choice. If they don't, and it creates a problem for you by being late to work, then put your helmet and flak jacket on and allow them to suffer the natural consequences listed above.

Follow through with what you have complete control over: the First National Bank of Mom and Dad being open or not; the "anytime you want" ride service being available or not; the "drop everything and get me, buy me, take me, give me" service; the "24-hour Mommy Maid" service; and the ever-popular, "I forgot it, but I know you'll get it for me" courier service.

You choose to keep these open or closed. Your kids have learned how to use whining, pouting, anger, temper tantrums and the like, in order to keep them open. Like a referee in an out-of-control game, blow the whistle and throw the flag on the field and call timeout.

To save your sanity, you, as a parent need to get off "the problem" as quickly as possible, and begin to step back and rethink that this is an opportunity for you to solve it another way. After this situation has occurred, and you both have time to discuss it, let them know that this situation creates two problems: you being late for work; and them being late for school.

Let them know you need their help in solving this problem. This will make them feel important and "powerful." That's what we want. Start by asking them what they think they can do to solve this problem. Give the ownership of it to them.

If they don't come up with a plan, then suggest buying a simple alarm clock. You'll probably have to teach them how to use it (we don't want to leave anything to chance). Explain that this is a problem they have complete control over, just like choosing when to go to bed, or what toys to play with.

Middle School

Typical Problem:

"My kids have a habit of lying to us. They lie about where they've been and what they've been doing. They lie about doing their homework. They lie about lots of things. What can I do?"

Practical Solution:

You know you don't own the problem, responsibility, decisions, power, control or choice for your children's lies. They own this problem. They can choose to tell the truth. They can choose to lie.

The most common reason why kids lie is to avoid what they think will happen if they tell the truth. This can be an opportunity for us as parents to step back and rethink about what kind of structure we've set up about telling the truth.

If kids know you'll yell, scream or generally lose it, when they own up to making poor choices, they'll choose what seems like the better option of lying. They won't understand the value of telling the truth.

This doesn't mean there should be no consequences for eventually telling the truth when they make poor choices. No, not at all! As the parent, you should set up a structure in your home that clearly states that they'll be respected and acknowledged for telling the truth, but will also be held accountable for the poor choices they make.

The consequences could be the loss of anything that's important to them. Just like in the above elementary school situation, they have total control over the consequences. If they demonstrate trustworthiness, not by what they say, but by what they do, they can earn back their privileges. Impress upon them that trustworthiness is a major part of your relationship with them. Let them know you believe they have the power, control and the choice to make better choices in the future.

Teaching and modeling to your kids that making the poor choice to lie isn't the end of the world will reinforce that telling the truth is the better option. Knowing you won't *react*, but that you'll rethink and turn a problem such as lying, as well as what they're lying about, into an opportunity for learning, will set a different tone for them to live by.

It will demonstrate that you know you don't have total control over the choices they make. But you do have the control over influencing them to be honest with you, and with others as well. You can influence them by sharing that being honest and trustworthy is a part of good character, and that being a person of good character is in their control.

High School

Typical Problem:

"My child is a high school athlete who said he's going to use tobacco, alcohol and other drugs, and there's nothing I can do about it. The school's athletic code prohibits these substances, but he said everybody at school thinks the code is a joke. The code apparently isn't working. What can I do?"

Practical Solution:

The code is only a "joke" if we as parents don't support it on the home-front. If our kids get even the slightest idea that we don't support the code, we foster their decision to not abide by it. Maybe you can't totally control what your son thinks about the code, but there is something you can do to INFLUENCE him in his decision to use or not use tobacco, alcohol or other drugs.

You have NO CONTROL over his ultimate choices, as frustrating as this may be, BUT you do have CONTROL over the choices YOU CAN MAKE regarding the consequences of his actions. You CONTROL setting up the structure and expectation in your home that he's not to use tobacco, alcohol and other drugs, regardless of whether there is or isn't a code of conduct (I certainly hope you agree with a NO USE policy here.)

No matter what rules or codes the school may adopt, you have the right as well as the legal structure, to establish and enforce rules for your kids regarding substance abuse, as long as they're living in your home and are under the legal age.

"But what if he won't follow these rules and insists on doing whatever he wants. What do I do then? I can't take things like the car, money or even athletics away from him because he'd lose his job, wouldn't have lunch money, and even lose out on athletics, which keeps him out of trouble in the first place."

At that point, step back and rethink about what your structure and expectations are for him, both on and off the field. If you expect him to not use tobacco, alcohol or other drugs, and you support the athletic policy (which you need to do), then the job loss is his problem, along with the closing of the First National Bank of Mom and Dad, and his participation in athletics.

It's not *your* problem unless you make it *your* problem. He'll learn that his poor choices cost him the use of the car. He'll learn to find other ways of getting around. He could walk, ride the bus, catch a ride with a friend or co-worker, or choose not to work at all.

He'll learn that if he wants something badly enough—being involved in athletics and getting you and others off his back—he'll be expected to make good choices, even when you or school officials aren't watching.

Unfortunately, many kids in these situations have learned what choices push your buttons the most. Over the years, they've probably learned to pout, whine, complain and even threaten to run away to get what they want. The problem is that, just like lures in the tackle box, these behaviors have worked for them on numerous occasions.

Influencing their attitudes and then their choices will take time and patience on your part. But if you put your helmet and flak jacket on, and not wimp out on me by watering down either your own structure or the school's code of conduct, then the outcome will certainly be worth the effort. You'll have kids who understand that structure is a part of life, and that they have the ability to make the right choices about following the structure.

If they choose not to follow it, then you choose to hold them accountable and support those setting the structure.

If you find evidence that suggests your son is using tobacco, alcohol or other drugs, despite the athletic code and any of your interventions suggested above, you need to tell him you expect him to inform the coach, the athletic director or another school official of his poor choices.

Give him the opportunity to do this by himself first and let him know you'll be calling the school at the end of the day to see if the athletic director has any questions. If your son didn't report his poor choices, you need to inform the athletic director, and promise your support of whatever enforce-ment decision is made.

If your child persists in using tobacco, alcohol or other drugs, it's a defi-nite sign that the use of these substances is more significant in his life than you realized. In that case, professional intervention may well be the next logical step for you to consider.

Rethinking from "No Choice" to CHOICES

UNLEASHING THE POWER OF CHOICE.
This is the Oscar-winning strategy that will
transform your life as a parent and
empower your kids!

"Old planet" choice?

Many kids, who grew up on the "old planet," believed choice was NO option. But, if you came right down to it, they did have a choice…Pick up your toys or **Else**; enjoy the vacation or **Else**; do the dishes or **Else**; do your chores or **Else**; do well in school or **Else**!

As you can imagine, **"Else"** was never clarified, discussed, or even thought about! **"Else"** was simply too frightening a thought! **"Else"** was enough of a choice for them. I suppose they could have chosen **"Else,"** but even the thought of the consequence was enough to keep you in line.

This doesn't mean the parents on the "old planet" were fascists or dictators, or anything close to that. When it came right down to it, **"Else"** was actually comforting for kids. They knew they had guidelines. They knew they had boundaries. They knew they had structure. The boundaries for behavior were clearly marked.

With that clarity also came safety from not having to make choices, because they were not options. For example, it wasn't an option to stay out past curfew; it wasn't an option to cut class or do badly in school; it wasn't an option to drink or use drugs! Those were simply **unshakable, unbreakable and non-negotiable!**

No one even had to say anything. There were no lectures. There were no rules posted on the walls. There were no assemblies to discuss this. The subtleties: like *"Thomsons don't do that,"* *"We'll be taking a short family break during school time, but our children will do their homework while they're* gone," "Honey, ladies and young men don't talk like that," or "You don't treat people like that," were imbedded in your brain. The most comforting thing was that you knew anything related to family, hard work, ethics, financial security, loyalty, and honesty were the **non-negotiables!**

So what happened? I've been asked that question a million times. I think that over the years the "new planet" kids have learned more and more about internal power, control and choices. "New planet kids" have learned they have the power of choice. Couple this with what they're seeing and hearing around them nowadays and you have kids who have learned how to co-opt their parents into believing that "Else" doesn't affect them as it did kids in the past. Just look around and you'll see what I mean.

Kids do want structure

If you were to ask adolescents on the "new planet" what they wished for, at the top of the list would probably be their desire to be left alone, given more space, more independence, more power, control and choice. What I've learned, not only from adolescents but from kids of all ages, is that along with these wishes, **kids want structure.**

As we mentioned above, structure gives them boundaries in which they can operate. Structure gives them a sense of security. What these "new planet" kids are saying sounds a lot like the "old planet" mentality described above, doesn't it?

The difference is that on the "old planet" these boundaries were clearly marked, both verbally and non-verbally by the "old planet" parents and, if you made a poor choice, parents not only huffed and puffed, but they followed through and blew the house down! Guaranteed.

Contrast that with parents I've observed today and you'll find huffing, puffing and just a bunch of threatening to blow the house down, with little or no follow through. And do you think the kids know this? You know the answer.

Let me repeat an important statement I made earlier: *"With that clarity also came safety from not having to make choices, because they were not options."* This is critical for us to learn from when dealing with our "new planet" kids.

Think about it: on the "old planet," there was more clarity regarding boundaries from adults, whether it was implied or not. "Old planet" parents stood up against evil things, people and situations because it was the right thing to do. And what really helped out "old planet" parents was that most kids followed their boundaries, believing it was the right thing to do—and if they didn't, **"Else"** happened!

Notice also that this clarity gave the kids "safety" from not having to make choices, because they weren't options. Many people who grew up in those days have commented that not having to make choices was actually comfortable for them. Even using their parents as an excuse for not making choices provided them safety.

As "new planet" parents, we need to step up to the plate and take from the "old planet" parents what worked in providing their kids with that safety net. Parents today need to be the ones who verbally and non-verbally set the structure. We need to be clear with our kids what we expect. We need to be clear with our kids what we'll do if they choose not to go by our expectations. This isn't a threat. It's just a promise to them that we'll be consistent— we will follow through.

As parents, we need to be the ones who provide our kids with the "safety net" of not only following the structure but also agreeing with the structure because it's the right thing to do. Kids today know they're flooded with a barrage of choices. What they've been telling me for years is that they want us to step in and provide them with clear expectations regarding what's acceptable and unacceptable behavior.

It's not only okay (but even advisable from our kids) for us to give our kids permission to use us as an excuse, or a "safety net," to make the right choice. There isn't a kid alive who hasn't "used" parents as an excuse for not doing something at some point. I say, fine with me. Do whatever it takes to make the right choices at the time.

Over the years, I've found you can either use the words "structure" or "expectations" with your kids. Notice I didn't use "rules," "control" or "power." Rules, in a young person's mind, means "you have to," "you must," or "you will." These words might have worked on the old planet, but not today.

Kids are more sophisticated today. They've challenged the "old planet" mentality. They know you don't "have to" do anything. They know they have choices. Using the words "structure" and "expectations" on the other hand, means quite the opposite to "new planet" kids. It connotes that they do have a choice—to follow or not follow the structure and expectations.

If they choose not to, they should understand that we'll be there to hold them accountable. If they choose to follow the structure and expectation, we'll be there to catch them making good choices. Either way, we're offering our children the power of choice. And that's what "new planet" kids have been telling me for years that they so desperately want.

With this chart in mind, sit down with your kids and discuss what your expectations are in your home, the school and the community, to name just a few

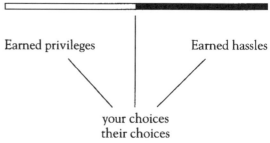

HOME EXPECTATIONS AGREEMENT

Earned privileges   Earned hassles

your choices
their choices

areas. Expecting proper behavior from children in the areas of cleaning their bedrooms, brushing their teeth, going to bed on time, waking up on time, treating other family members with respect, abiding by curfew, not using tobacco, alcohol or other drugs, obtaining good grades, attending school, and behaving at school, is entirely reasonable.

Once you've shared with your kids what you believe are your structure or expectations in these areas, allow them to have input. This gives them a sense of ownership. Allow them to disagree with your structure or expectations, and let them express their own feelings.

After listening to their side, you might agree that some areas might be open to change or adjustment. On the other hand, some may not be. Allow your kids to come up with their ideas that might make the expectations reasonable and fair. You may be amazed at how reasonable their suggestions will be.

Thomas Jefferson once wrote: *"In matters of style, swim with the current; in matters of principle, stand like a rock."* That's good advice. Many principles of yours may be unshakable and unbreakable. Naturally you have the final choice of what the structure will be and what's expected, as far as your children's behavior goes. But I really believe going through this process with your kids will teach them that the real world is all about structure, expectations, opinions, choices, and the outcome of those choices—and, most importantly, that the choices are theirs to make.

Good choice, poor choice, my choice

The phrase: "Good Choice, Poor Choice, My Choice," needs to be stamped on your kids' foreheads! It needs to be on the walls in their bedroom. It needs to be prominently displayed where you, and they, can see it clearly. This is an incredibly powerful phrase—for your kids, and for you as parents.

With this phrase as our backdrop, we need to create a vision in our kids' head that in most of life they have the power of choice. This allows *them* to have control over making good choices or poor choices. Success in life is in the good choices they make. Failure in life is in the poor choices they make. Either way, they need to understand that they always have "the power of choice."

Knowing this puts us in a great position to teach and model to our kids that problems are the result of poor choices made, at the time. I say "at the time" because, if we're really honest with ourselves, we too have said or done some really dumb, stupid things "at the time" in our lives.

Do you agree? Acknowledging that our kids are going to make poor choices "at the time" should be our signal to not react but rethink. This is an opportunity for us to help our kids step back, rethink about the problem, responsibility, decisions, power, control and choices, focusing on what choices were made at the time, and what choices we can teach them to consider making next time.

Thinking this way will keep us as parents from "reacting" that our kids are "bad" for the choices they're making. They aren't bad kids; they're just making poor choices "at the time." Also by becoming the teacher and model of "better choices," it puts us in a position to step back and rethink that we have an opportunity to help our children evaluate their choices made at the time.

Instead of dwelling on the poor choices they may have made (which is something in the past and now out of their control), we can help them evaluate those choices, identify the consequences they may have paid, and brainstorm alternative choices for the future.

Our daughter Holly provided a classic example of "Good Choice, Poor Choice, My Choice." It was 8:30 on a Sunday evening and bedtime around our house. My wife Carol and I gave the *"It's time to go to bed"* call to both our kids. Holly, who was then in second grade, began to walk toward the stairs, then froze like a deer caught in headlights, gasped for breath, sighed, rolled her eyes, and started saying, *"Oh no, I have a project due for school tomorrow!"*

In a frantic voice, she said to us, *"I need poster paper, stickers, paste, glue, and scissors!"* To which we replied, *"What, did the teacher just call you on the phone tonight and tell you about this?"* Holly responded with a drawn out *"No...."* Our answer: *"You and your buddy Emily had an awesome weekend. You got A's in sleep over, A's in video rental, A's in phone time, A's in Barbie Dolls, A's in riding your bike and A's in hang out, but you need to go to bed right now. We don't do homework after 8:30."*

Holly immediately came back with, *"You have to go out and get me my stuff!"* (Hint: these are lures in her attempt to get *you* to take on the problem). After we spit out that lure, she tried another one, *"You'd have gone to the store for Chris!"* When that failed, she stomped three steps further and tried the world-famous: *"You love Chris more."* Getting no reaction, she finished stomping up the stairs and threw herself into bed, throwing out one "last hurrah" lure: *"Thanks a lot, you're going to make me fail!"* and then pulled the covers over her head!

Can you picture this scene? When the dust settled, my wife and I looked at each other in a somewhat perplexed way. I think we both had the passing thought of jumping in the car, driving to the all-night store, huffing and puffing up and down the aisles, swearing under our breath about how irresponsible Holly was.

Not this time! We'd been beaten up too many times before in similar situations. Instead, we held our ground and told her: *"It's bedtime right now. You know we don't do school work at this time of night. You had enough time to do it over the weekend. When you get to school tomorrow, you need to let your teacher know that you chose not to do your project and that you're choosing to suffer the consequences for your poor choices."*

Holly cried hysterically and attempted to trap us into believing *we* were responsible for her getting into trouble with her teacher. By the way, the hysterical crying and the accusations are also lures in her attempt to get *us* to take on the problem.

It was about that time that I developed the "Who Owns the Problem" poster. When Holly was under the covers, I stepped back and said to her: *"We're going to make you fail? Wait just a minute here. Who Owns the Problem? Who Owns the Responsibility? Who Owns the Decisions? Who Has the Power? Who Has the Control? Who Makes the Choices?*

As I paused after each of these questions, I could hear Holly under the covers, snorting like a buck in the woods! It was clear to me that she definitely knew the answers to these questions, and so did I.

Holly saw us as "the worst parents" for not running out and getting her the stuff for her project, and for letting her get into trouble with her teacher. I could almost see the pouting lures, the temper lures, and the ever-popular crying lure coming out of her "tackle box," in her attempts to get us to own the problem.

She used all those behavioral lures, hoping for a bite. My wife and I felt tempted, particularly when she used the guilt lure that had caught us many a time in the past, but we didn't give in. We spit each lure out as it was cast our way. It was tough, but we chose not to give in. It was the last time we can think of that Holly was ever late for *her* projects or homework.

Can you relate to getting sucked in by your kids like this? Can you think of other situations where you allowed your child to place responsibility for his or her poor choices on you or someone else? Can you use *"The Six Critical Questions"* the next time your children try to "hook" you with one of their choice behaviors?

The bottom line here is that I want you to avoid solving problems *for* your kids. It just gives them the impression that every time something goes wrong, someone else will step in and fix the problem for them. This results in postponing accountability for who owns the problem.

Remember what I've stated before: 98 percent of all problem situations won't kill you or your kids. It's okay if they get frustrated with a problem. That's life. This doesn't mean, of course, that you can't do things for your kids once in awhile to help out. But the sooner you allow your children to accept responsibility for their own actions, thoughts and feelings, the sooner you'll have kids who act responsibly when frustration arises, whether you're there or not.

You're all done grounding your kids!

Don't get sucked into the "Thanks a lot for grounding me" trap by your kids. Spit this lure out as quickly as your kids cast it. As soon as you hear it, you need to help them step back and rethink by influencing them with what I call the "velvet hammer "question: *"Am I the one who grounded you, or was it the poor choice you made at the time?"*

Here's another interesting way of helping your kids rethink the issue of grounding. Ask them: *"If you choose to come in on time, treat people in the house with respect, take care of your responsibilities around the house and at school, and generally make good choices, would those choices get us more on your back or off your back?"* *"And if you make these good choices, would it be fair for us to ground you?"* *"So who's really grounding whom?"*

Once you understand that *you* will never take anything away from your kids, but that their poor choices will, life will take on such a different meaning. You'll feel less stress. You'll feel so powerful! Knowing your kids are choosing their earned privileges, as well as their earned hassles, allows you the freedom to NOT take on their problems.

Oh, what a relief this is! **It also allows you the opportunity to teach your children that they "earn" hassles,** such as sitting in their bedroom, going to bed early, being without their treasured toy, television, stereo, the phone, or the use of the car, their bike, or a ride from you, to name just a few.

And the key is, you guessed it, nobody took these away from them. It had to do entirely with the choices they made "at the time." Again, velvet hammer questions such as, *"What was the expectation or rule you made a choice to break?" "What poor choices did you make to earn yourself the hassles you're getting?" "What better choices could you make next time?"* will definitely influence your kids' thinking in the right way. **Allow your kids time to sit and rethink about the choices they made at the time, as it pertains to the consequences they're suffering as a result.**

During this rethinking time period, let your kids know they can earn back the lost privileges when *they* are ready to discuss this problem with you. This is your time to keep that *"Who Owns the Problem"* poster prominently displayed anywhere you can see it. This is your time to keep humming the "Good Choice, Poor Choice, My Choice" phrase.

This is also your time to step back, rethink, and focus on who owns the problem, responsibility, decisions, power, control and choices. It's your time to keep a calm and direct tone of voice with your kids when discussing this problem. And this is the time to remember it's "their problem," not yours. Don't for a second wimp out here! Don't get sucked into taking on their problem, responsibility, decisions, power, control and choices. Don't do it!

These "velvet hammer" questions will motivate your children to rethink about the choices they're making in life. They're the "salt in the horse's oats" that will influence them to think differently about the problem they're in. Helping them think differently about problems is one of your roles as a parent.

The best part here is that you'll be controlling in asking the questions, but not in getting a response. In fact, your kids don't even have to answer them. That's why they're so great. They're like a time-release capsule. They just influence your thinking. What a difference just asking them will make.

If you don't believe me, you can always try the other way, the threatening, voice-raising method, but after years of doing this myself, I can tell you it just isn't worth it. The prices outweigh the rewards.

Okay, now that I have you asking some great "velvet hammer" questions, the million-dollar question you probably have is, "How long is it going to take for our kids to take responsibility for their poor choices?" Here's the gazillion dollar answer….I don't know!

The reason I don't know is that we don't have total control over our kids' thoughts, actions or feelings. We don't own the problem and we're not the ones with the power of choice to make changes. Our kids are. So the only answer I can give you is that you'll begin to notice change with time. Time that you allow your kids to be without their privileges. Time that you allow your kids to sit and rethink about their problem, responsibility, decisions, power, control and choices made.

Only time to rethink about these questions will change a negative attitude. Only time to rethink about these questions will influence a person's thinking. Only time being without something they want will motivate them to change. In fact, how badly your kids want what they want will determine how much effort they put into answering these questions and changing their attitude or actions. It may take some time, but getting back whatever they lost out on is up to them, not you.

Get me, buy me, take me, give me!

Unfortunately, we're surrounded by a large number of lazy children today with the middle name of **"get me, buy me, take me, give me."** Get me what I want. Buy me what I want. Take me where I want to go. Give me whatever I want. And if you don't, I'll make life miserable for you!

You know as well as I do that going out and getting it, buying it, taking them or giving them will not promote hard work, ethics, or loyalty to the family, or anyone else for that matter. What happened to us? How did we become so wimpy? And how did our kids become so powerful?

Consider the story of a mother with two teenage sons who have attitude problems, do poorly in school both academically and behaviorally, and generally make a lot of poor choices. But they always get what they want from Mom. Mom puts up a good fight from time to time, threatening to ground them, but never follows through (the old "huff, puff, and threaten to blow the house down" syndrome.)

She threatens to not drive them where they want to go, but always gives in. She threatens to let them be late for school, but then drives them anyway and hands them an excuse because they demand one. She threatens to pull privileges from them, but gives in when they scream, pout, whine or threaten to make life even more miserable for her (which is really hard to imagine how that could be much worse than the reality she's living now.)

What these kids have learned at a young age has been how to "control" Mom. These kids have found out what "lures" they need to use on Mom to hook her into the get me, buy me, take me, give me game. And from what we see here, the sons' lures have worked!

Take this story one step further and you'll find these kids blaming Mom for all their problems, with statements such as, *"You made me late for school." "It will be your fault if I get a detention or a bad grade." "How come you didn't wake me up?" "You should have reminded me about the test."* What these statements represent are great excuses (fostered by Mom's getting, buying, taking and giving) for the two sons to not accept responsibility for their own choices.

Look back on the blaming statements being made by these kids. See the word "you" come up a lot? You made me. You didn't. You should have. It's your fault. Blamers love to focus on "out there" and in this case "Mom" as the cause of "their" problems. And as long as Mom takes on the two sons' problems, responsibility, decisions, power, control and choices, she will deserve the blame. Mom has allowed the kids to do this to her.

Mom needs to throw the flag on the field and call time out! She needs to take control of the blame game and set down the structure from this point forward. It won't be easy. But it's not easy now. Mom needs to grab the "Who Owns the Problem" poster and drill it into her head that she is all done taking on her sons' problems, responsibility, decisions, power, control and choices.

From this point forward, if her kids choose not to get out of bed on time for school, that's a problem she's going to turn over to them. She'll get them an alarm clock, so they get up on their own. If they don't, there are usually consequences for getting to school late. Mom won't be writing excuses anymore and will inform school officials when her sons are at home without her permission. Mom will inform her sons that she will support the school in whatever disciplinary action is taken

If these two sons are typical, they'll attempt to verbally beat down and blame Mom for these consequences, but Mom quickly remembers the "Who Owns the Problem" poster, and chooses not to get sucked into this. Mom also lets them know that if they refuse to follow through with responsibilities at school, they'll suffer the loss of additional privileges at home. These are all a result of "their poor choices" in not following through with their responsibilities.

On the lecture circuit, I often mention that when my kids started third grade, part of their routine was to get themselves up with their own alarm clocks, make their lunches, pick out their clothes, clean up their rooms, pick up their messes, make their breakfast, and do their homework. Some people in the audience have questioned me about this, and wondered if it's okay to allow children to do so much for themselves.

It sure beats shaking them in bed, yelling up the stairs for the "last" time, bribing them to do their chores, threatening them with empty ultimatums, fixing the "wrong food" for their breakfast or lunch, picking out the clothes "I" like and they hate, and so on.

My wife and I found that it naturally became a source of relief for us as parents, and a tremendous source of pride and power for our children. The earlier you start handing over responsibility the better.

Which would you rather hear from your kids; "I love you because you talk with me, spend time with me, read to me, listen to me, really care about me and teach me responsibility," or "I love you because you get me up in the morning, make my lunch for me, buy clothes for me, pick out my clothes for me, give me money, remind me about what I have to do each day and take on my responsibilities?"

I'm convinced in observing my own kids, as well as other kids, that the more your children realize you will do what they want if they whine, pout, complain or have a temper tantrum, and say things such as *"I give up,"* or *"I can't do it,"* the more they believe the responsibility for life's tasks rests with you.

And, trust me on this one, the older they get, the more difficult it becomes to change your children's "learned helplessness." It's not impossible, but more difficult. They will become like the fisherman, using their best pouting, whining, complaining and anger lures in order to "catch" you, and manipulate you into doing what they want. If they've been catching fish with those lures for years, why would they want to change?

We need to teach our kids that they have the power and the control to make good choices in their life. If they make poor choices that result in problems, then they need to be taught by us to look at how "they own the problem and responsibility" for the decisions they make, as well as how to step back, rethink and focus on this as an opportunity.

It's an opportunity to look at the choices they have 100 percent control over, from this point forward. If we fail to teach this while they're in our home, the result will be young adults who tell us their boss is a jerk for reprimanding them for being late, or for eventually firing them, that the cop is a jerk for picking them up for speeding, and that the professor is responsible for their poor grades. Poppycock!

KEY POINTS TO REMEMBER

- Punishment doesn't teach a person what to do as much as it teaches a person what not to do.
- Punishment subtly teaches a person that someone "out there" has more power, control and choices than the one who's being punished does.
- Think of kids as little horses you're trying to train. You can lead a horse to water, and even though it might not drink, you can salt the oats to increase its interest.
- Teach children that when they have a problem in their lives, they own the responsibility, decisions, power, control and choices for solving it.
- It's important to take a stand against evil people and situations because it's the right thing to do.
- Pay attention to the "get me, buy me, take me, give me" child, by not allowing the demanding to take over your rational thinking.
- Kids want and need structure from us. Structure provides our kids with a "safety net" to make the right choices even when we're not watching.
- Set the structure by establishing clear expectations, and allowing your children to earn the privileges and the hassles for their choices.
- You will never "take" anything away from your kids. Their poor choices will do that for them.
- Allow kids to gain independence in their lives through the choices they make.
- Teach your kids they can make good choices as well as poor choices, but that they always have the power of choice.
- Allow your kids the opportunity to sit without a privilege for as long as it takes for them to work their way through *"The Six Critical Questions."*
- Remember to not fall into the "get me, buy me, take me, give me" trap with your kids.

AREAS TO PRACTICE AND SHARE

Ask yourself two questions:
1. Am I doing this now?   *2. Am I going to start doing this?*

- When your kids make poor choices, make sure you provide opportunities for them to demonstrate that they can make better ones in the future.
- Provide opportunities for your kids to have input on your structure/expectations.
- Allow your kids the opportunity to discuss additional privileges they might be able to earn, as well as the choices they'll need to make in order to gain these extra privileges.
- Provide your children the opportunity to openly discuss whatever they want with you. Allow them to express their opinions openly and honestly without reprisal from you for doing so. This will open up the pearly gates of communication faster than you can finish this sentence.
- Be willing to hold your children accountable for their choices, even if it creates some change in your plans.
- Teach and model to your children that the world is filled with wonderful opportunities to make choices. These choices can be good choices or poor choices, but they're always their choices to make.
- Discuss with your kids that people should not be viewed as either good or bad. Help them rethink that it's the person's *behavior* that's in question at the time.
- Make a plan to discuss with your kids current situations in the news that are a result of people making either good choices or poor choices. Identify the positive and/or negative consequences for the choices made.
- Sit down with your kids and discuss *The Six Critical Questions.* Be prepared to offer them examples of when people in your life, when you were growing up, may have taken on your problems, responsibility, decisions, power, control and choices. Discuss the pros and cons of this and how it fostered victimhood and blamehood or adulthood behavior on your part.
- Sit down with your kids and discuss your most important home, school, or community expectations regarding their behavior when in those environments. Examples may include cleaning up their bedrooms, getting themselves up for school, putting away their own possessions, an agreed upon performance in school, time for bed, curfew, attitude, language, and no tobacco, alcohol or other drugs.

Typical Problems...Dr. Mike's Practical Solutions

Insert the problem here.

WHO owns the
PROBLEM?

WHO owns the
RESPONSIBILITY?

WHO made the
DECISIONS?

WHO has the
POWER?

WHO has the
CONTROL?

WHO makes the
CHOICES?

CHARACTER

©Michael M. Thomson Ph.D. 1995

Pre-School/Elementary School

Typical Problem:

"We've been using 'time out' as a way of trying to correct our son. Sometimes he throws a fit and fights all the way up to his room. Sometimes he just goes up there without a care in the world. Either way, when he comes out of the room, he's mad at me and we seem to not talk to each other for quite some time. Help!"

Practical Solution:

My mother used to send me up to my room for "time out." That concept has been used forever and a day. The problem for me wasn't time out. The problem was that when I was up in my room, I kept thinking about how my mother was being mean to me and was being unfair. I also didn't know whether to stay up there until I was 87, or come down in a few minutes.

Eventually, I came down the stairs, slid into the kitchen, and my mother asked me: *"And did you think about what you did wrong?"* Well, what idiot would say *"No!"*? I wanted to get back out there in the real world, so I remember saying something like, *"Yeah, okay, I'm sorry,"* when I really wasn't.

The time your child spends in time out shouldn't be a "jail sentence" to be served. It should be thought of as an opportunity for your child to calm down, step back and rethink about the "poor choices" he made that warranted him "choosing" to be in time out.

Notice I use the word "choosing" here in quotation marks. I do this because I believe this is your opportunity to teach your child responsibility for the poor choice that brought about the time out. He needs to understand it wasn't you, or anyone else, who sent him to his room. It was his poor choice that earned him the time out.

As to how long your child should be in time out, a good rule of thumb is a minute for every year of the child's age up until five, then no more than twenty minutes. I always found that while they were sitting there, they needed to answer three questions before they returned to their normal routine: 1) What was the structure or expectation you made a choice to break? 2) What poor choice did you make? 3) What better choice could you make next time?

Middle School

Typical Problem:
"My middle school child has friends who've been known to use alcohol and or other drugs. Should I be concerned about her? What should I say or do?"

Practical Solution:
You do have something to be worried about here, even if your daughter isn't directly involved with the use of these substances. Drug and alcohol use and abuse is one of the most serious problems affecting our teens today. It's very important that we set down a serious structure with our kids that we expect them not to get involved with alcohol or other drugs. We need to provide them with numerous choices they can use in saying no ("I hate the taste," "My parents will kill me," "I'll be grounded for life!" or "Thanks, but no thanks.")

The worst mistake you can make is to say or do nothing when this situation comes up. Sticking your head in the sand and hoping it's just a phase and will just go away doesn't work. In fact, doing nothing is a message to your kids that this issue isn't important. And since the issue of alcohol and other drugs is a part of the "evil" behaviors we've already discussed you need to take a stand against it. You need to be heard regarding your preference for your kids to be alcohol and drug free. Your structure on this strong expectation should be unshakable and unbreakable.

Make it clear to your kids that the consequences for them going against this structure will include you stepping in on their life and controlling their going out or not, their curfew, their privileges, their participation in school-related activities, and so forth. If you're willing to put your helmet and flak jacket on and stand your ground with your unshakable and unbreakable structure on this issue, the outcome for both you and your kids will be one you'll both appreciate in the long run.

High School

Typical Problem:
"I overheard my kids talking about 'freak dancing,' which I later found out is dancing that mimics various explicit sexual positions while on the dance floor. I know many kids want to be popular and be a part of the 'in' crowd, but I think this kind of dancing is degrading and disgraceful. What should I say or do?"

Practical Solution:
Some people will say freak dancing, or whatever the "dance of the month club" creates as the latest fad, is just an expression of adolescence. Okay, let's go with that. It's an expression all right. But, in my opinion, it's an expression that drags the images of kids down to the lowest level. I want kids to know I believe they can make a positive difference in the world today, even in the area of dancing. They can demonstrate to others that they can be better than that which is being played out on television or in print media as the "in" thing to do.

Here are a couple of suggestions I have for opening up dialogue with your kids on this one. Ask them if the image of freak dancing will portray them or other young people today in a positive or negative manner. Ask them if they want people to form perceptions of them as being sexually loose, or easy. After all, like it or not, this is the perception most people watching this dance will form of those doing it.

Ask your kids if dancing like this will either enhance or hurt a person's reputation? Ask them if they'd like significant others, such as grandparents, brothers or sisters, relatives, teachers, coaches or members of the clergy, to see a picture of them on the front page of the newspaper doing this dance? These are "velvet hammer" questions that whack them on the side of the head in a nice but firm fashion. These questions provide the "influence" you can make on your child's behavior.

Even with influencing questions such as these, your child might come back and say something like, *"It's just dancing, what's the big deal? It's not like it's going to lead to sex."* This is your opportunity to step back, rethink and calmly get into discussions with them about what you expect of them as a son or a daughter, and also as a young lady or young man as they grow up.

Explain to them that you know from experience that there's a difference between girls and young ladies, and boys and young men. A boy will be looking for a girl who's easy, loose and what's referred to by many rude and crude names by today's adolescents. These are what boys refer to as the "one night stand" girls. Just the labels they get placed on them by others for their choices ought to be a signal.

Boys will look for girls like this and vice versa. Dancing like this will be like an animal leaving its scent on every tree it passes. This "scent" will be attracting animals, which have no control over their sexual cravings. They just do it. And just like many animals, they leave right after conception.

That's what separates us from the animals. We have control. A young man and a young lady know the choices they demonstrate will attract what they're looking for. They know they have control over how they want others to perceive them. They know the choices they make will be a reflection of that perception.

As you've probably guessed by now, I firmly believe "freak dancing" is wrong. I know it's a problem and a choice I have no control over, but I can influence it with what I say and what I do.

It's the "evil" I've been talking about that we need to step in on. It's a problem that I think we as adults have the responsibility for stepping in on, in a calm and dignified manner. We need to let ourselves be heard—by our kids, and by others who are influencing our kids. Enough said!

Rethinking from "Controlling" to RELATIONSHIP

CREATING THE SIMPLE PATH to a successful relationship between you and your kids that will last a lifetime!

You're not the boss of me!

"What do you mean, 'you're not the boss of me' ... I'm your father ... I'm your mother. You'll do what I say or else! Get over here this instant! You must respect me. I demand that you do what I say! I brought you into this world and I'll take you out! And I don't mean for pizza!"

Can you relate to saying any of these to your kids? If you can, then you fall into the category of people who've been taught to think wrong. For some reason, you (and millions of other people) have bought into the belief that you have total control over how your kids should think, act and feel.

Unfortunately, this will set you up as a controlling type of person. **Once you fall into this type of thinking, you'll believe you can *force* others to behave the way you want them to, just by what you say or do.** Good luck!

In some cases, controlling choices on your part may work. But in most cases, today's children know control better than we did at their ages. The more you try to control them, the more they control you. They can beat you up psychologically, with expressions such as: *"You can't make me." "You're not the boss of me." "I can do whatever I want to."*

In the past, on the old planet, parents met very little resistance from their children. Kids did what they were asked to do. The new planet kids bring with them a new mentality regarding the issue of control, along with a new set of problems to tackle. Let's look at some ways for you to tackle these issues, and save your sanity in the meantime.

In my on-stage presentations, I have the audience raise their right hands and show me their palm. I tell them to put that hand on the back of the head and wiggle their fingers, while looking at the person on their left and then on their right. They all laugh and wonder what they're doing. I inform them that these wiggling fingers are what I call "choice detectors" or "challenge detectors."

On the old planet, those "choice detectors" were in a person's pocket. Back then, you might have thought about going against what was expected of you, and challenging the norm, but that's as far as you went. Your thoughts never became actions. You were the original "legend in your own mind" poster child. If you talked back to adults the way some kids do today, most of you wouldn't have been able to sit down for weeks!

I'm convinced that out of one hundred children on the old planet, about ninety-nine towed the line. They had the choice detectors in their pockets, playing with their spare change. Today, I believe the opposite is true, with those choice detectors up and waving.

Gaining control through punishment?

How should we deal with these kids who know they have these "choice detectors?" What about using punishment? Does it work with today's kids? Is it okay to hit, to spank, and to threaten? What do we teach our kids by hitting them, kicking them, throwing things at them, or threatening them with physical harm?

It worked for some parents on the old planet—and their parents. Or did it? Should we keep on using these tactics? How severe is too severe? If it doesn't work at 20 mph, should we go to 40 mph? Or maybe even 100 mph if we have to? So many questions to answer.

Punishment has been around for a long time. There are even verses in the Bible that allude to the need for punishment, or the need for "correction" of the child who disobeys. "The Old Woman in the Shoe" story states that when the kids were bad, she "whipped them soundly and put them to bed." Many believe in punishment as the only form of discipline that works with kids. Others disagree.

Punishment isn't usually effective, for several reasons. First, it teaches a person what "not to do," instead of "what to do." It's more concerned with stopping a behavior than looking at other choices to rethinking the problem at hand. Punishment isn't primarily concerned with teaching better choices but with control. In fact, punishment is attempting to control another person, period!

Second, to be effective, punishment needs to be immediate and severe. In some cases, it does work, which quite frankly is the worst thing that can happen.

Let me explain. We spank, hit, physically threaten and control our children, to let them know "who's in charge." It becomes the worst thing that can happen if it's reinforced through success. We see that making these choices works to "correct" the child and we feel this is the best choice for getting what we want.

Third, I think punishment teaches a child that someone "out there" has more power, control and choices than they do. I DO NOT want your kids to think this way. I want your kids to know they have a tremendous amount of power, control and choices in life.

When punishment works, it produces in parents what I call the "blowfish syndrome." Just like a blowfish, we swell up with what we think is **power over others**, leading us further into the illusion of control. In the end, what we accomplish indirectly is to teach our children that control through punishment works.

We really begin to think we're omnipotent. Raising the volume, getting our eyes to bug out, and popping our veins are all ways we use to try and "control" our children's behavior. If any or all of these choices work, we continue to use them—time after time after time.

But I want you to rethink with me that, if kids learn to behave the way "we want them to" out of fear of punishment, they'll never learn how to behave normally without us around them. They'll only get sore necks from twisting and turning to see if we're listening or watching them.

The television show "20/20" did an excellent program on discipline, in which the researchers pointed out that in the long run punishment doesn't work. They found out that punishment doesn't help people develop into who we want them to be. In a twenty-year follow-up study of parents who had used punishment as their form of discipline at home, they found the following to be true:

- Punished kids were arrested more often.
- Punished kids suffered more depression.
- Punished kids did worse academically.
- Punished kids earned less money.
- Punished kids had more difficulties in relationships.
- Punished kids tended to not like themselves.

From what we see here, punishment is not only ineffective, it actually produces the opposite of what people want. People want control through punishment. What we've learned through this research study is that punishment produced and fostered loss of control.

This puts you in a position to teach and model to your kids that getting physical with another person doesn't prove anything. In fact, it just brings one more problem into your life, on top of whatever you want to solve. Teach and model to your kids that the real strength is between your ears, and knowing when to hold back any type of violence between you and another person.

Do you agree with what we've said here? What are some of the prices you or others have paid in letting emotions and not brains take over the decision at the time?

Obviously we need to go beyond punishment. We need to begin to create, within our own minds, the vision that all people are capable of making both good and poor choices at the time. If we can understand that people are always making their best choice(s) at the time, it will make us teachers of better choices when problems arise.

We won't view our kids or others as bad people, but simply as people making poor choices at the time. This statement may sound a little confusing, but stop for a minute and think about the last time you made what you considered to be a good choice at the time, then moments later said to yourself, *"What a dumb thing to do."*

Have you made some choices like this at the time? What about those times you said or did something you regretted later? Perhaps you evaluated that choice and decided it wasn't such a great one after all. If you were "punished" every time you made poor choices, would that help you learn, or would you get angry over being punished by someone with greater power?

Control meets control

Parents are confronted with situations where they want their children to behave in certain ways. It starts out in the morning with, *"Get out of bed, it's time for school,"* followed by, *"I'm only going to say this one more time, you're going to be late,"* or, *"I have to be at work right now and you haven't even dressed yet,"* and continues after school with, *"You have to do your homework now,"* *"You'd better be in this house on time or you'll get it,"* or, *"Go to bed this minute."*

When these requests fall on deaf ears, many parents yell a little louder in order to be heard and obeyed. Getting no response, they yell louder and the kids continue to disobey. The frustration level rises with each attempt. The inevitable occurs: **Parent Burnout!**

Parents will burn out when they want control over things, people or situations they have no control over. Obviously in the above situations, the parents have a right to want what they want from their kids. The reality is that parents only have "influence" over getting their kids to make the right choices and do what they want.

When parents aren't getting what they want from their kids, they tend to resort to controlling measures to try and make their kids behave the way they want them to. Unfortunately, the more parents attempt to control their kids, and their attempts don't work, the more out of control parents become.

Often, during my travels around the country, I've asked kids if they've ever heard one or more of the following, when their parents are trying to **"get them"** to do something:

"You're going to do it because it's the rule around here, that's why!"
"Because I said so, that's why!"
"Because I'm your mother, that's why!"
"Because I'm your father, that's why!"
"Because I'm the adult and you're the child."
"Fine, don't do what I say ...you just wait until your father gets home!"
"Okay (holding out fingers) ... one ... two ... if I get to three, that little butt of yours is going to shine!"

The kids go wild when I ask if they've ever heard these statements made by their parents—they raise their hands, and even their feet! This tells me that parents today are using choices many of their parents used on them on the "old planet" in their attempts to make kids behave the way they want them to. And what you'll hear from parents is that they have to turn up the volume in order to gain more control of their kids.

Unfortunately, many parents have confirmed that when they raised their voice, threatened or even physically grabbed their kids, their kids did what they wanted. I say unfortunately, because this behavior on the parents' part creates a perception in their kids' minds that the parents have more power, control and choices.

Hence the perception is created in the kids' minds that they have "controlling" parents. And trust me on this one, being a controlling person is something you don't want in your life as a parent. It will just create more problems for you.

Let me give you an example. Tom and Suzy had a problem with their son Tony, who was coming in late for curfew, not doing his homework, skipping school, and treating his parents with disrespect. When they came to my office, I knew immediately that something was up. The parents sat on one side of the waiting room, while Tony sat on the other, with his chair turned completely away from them.

Here's what I quickly noticed about Tony. He was wearing about forty pounds of earrings on one ear, was dressed all in black, with strategic tears in his jeans, hair shaved on one side and what looked like two feet of hair on the other, the numbers 666 inked on his knuckles, along with "Hail Satan" scribbled in pencil on his notebook, which he proudly displayed. I ushered them all into my office and opened with the typical, *"Tell me what brings you here today."*

With that, Tom proceeded to tell me in a very angry, controlling voice that his son was nothing but a *"dirtball and no good lazy bum."* He went on to list the various things that frustrated him about his son and how he was one problem after another. The list seemed never ending.

To speed things along, and to prevent Tom from foaming at the mouth, I decided to ask Suzy for her input. Sitting quietly, she whispered, *"I think Tom has said it best."*

I then leaned toward Tony and asked him for his perception of the problem. He refused to answer my question, and proceeded to snap his gum loudly and just stare at his Dad. Dad just about hit the roof. He began yelling at Tony, telling him: *"This is costing me money, you'd better talk,"* to which Tony just shrugged his shoulders and smiled.

In order to avoid an all-out war, I asked the parents to return to the waiting room. Back in the office with Tony, I began to try and sift through the situation. At first he said nothing, but just stared into space. I went up to the board and wrote down the following four characteristics of healthy families:

1. PERMISSION TO TALK
2. PERMISSION TO DEMONSTRATE TRUST
3. PERMISSION TO SHARE FEELINGS
4. PERMISSION TO DEMONSTRATE LOYALTY

When I asked if he's given permission to talk in his family, he blurted out, *"What do you think?"* I replied, *"I'm going to take a wild guess and say you don't get a chance to talk much, is that right?"* Tony said, *"You're a real rocket scientist, aren't you?"* To which I said: *"That's part of that psychology training they put me through; you get books with it too!"*

I asked Tony if he could trust or be trusted, and he said, *"They don't trust me and I don't trust them. So what?"* When asked about his feelings, he was quick to point out that he had a lot of feelings about what was going on. He hated the controlling, hated the criticism, the arguments, and the threatening by his Dad.

Now that we were talking about his problems and I was beginning to build a relationship with him, I asked him the question I was dying to ask. I wanted to know about his choice of black clothing, the 666 on his knuckles, and the "Hail Satan" written on his notebook. I knew this style has been connected to satanic rituals and the like.

I asked Tony if he was into this, and he boldly replied, *"Heck no, I'm not into that crap."* I responded with, *"Then why do you display this so much?"* to which he said, *"Because it just bugs the hell out of my Dad!"* This statement just blew me away! It proved to me that Tony was no more into the satanic belief system than the man in the moon.

It also taught me that "choice behaviors" on Tony's part are purposeful ones. They're choices Tony uses to control his controlling Dad. Tony clearly stated that the more he was controlled by his father to think, act and feel the way his father wanted, the more he controlled him back, hence the choices in his behavior.

How are you perceived by your kids?

For a moment, think of me as a positive, friendly, fun kind of person. Think of me as the type of person you'd really like to get to know. What will you do? How will you feel? If you meet me, will you move toward me? Will you move away from me? If you think of me as a negative, hostile, critical person, controlling person, what will you do? How will you feel? Will you move toward me? Will you move away from me?

If you see me as a positive person, you'll probably move toward me. If you see me as a negative person, you'll probably move away from me. What causes you to move toward or away from me? Is it what I do? No. **What causes you to move toward or away from me is how you choose to think of me. Your thoughts will direct your actions to move toward or away from another person.**

In my parenting seminars, I have the parents look at what makes them approachable, and what makes them unapproachable, in their day-to-day life with their kids. It's amazing how perceptive parents are if they put themselves in the role of their children and honestly answer the questions: *"Do my kids think of me as approachable?"* *"Do I give my kids permission to express their thoughts and their feelings?"* *"Do my kids perceive me as need fulfilling or need reducing?"*

These questions give parents valuable information in evaluating their kids' perceptions of them. Having this information regarding your kids' perceptions will help you determine whether they're motivated to move toward you or away from you. This kind of evaluation can help you decide what you need to do to influence your kids in a more positive and productive manner.

Now think about this. What actions do you choose to use that just "irritate the bejeebers out of your kids?" Are you willing to ask your kids or your spouse what actions could be on this list? Would you accept their answers without being defensive about it?

If you give your kids the impression that you're open to receiving this information from them, you'll be setting up an atmosphere where it's permissible for family members to talk about their feelings regarding each other in a constructive, non-critical, informative fashion.

You might hear things such as: *"Mom, when you tell me to do my homework, you just keep yelling at me at the top of your lungs in a negative, critical tone that really bugs me."* *"Dad, you're always on my back about the clothes I wear or the style of my hair—what's the big deal about these anyway?"*

The typical parent would "react" and say something like: *"Don't you talk to me like that, I'm your Mother (or your Father), I know what's right for you; now get going and do what I say!"* But from what we're seeing here, you know we don't need to "react" to these comments like this. We can choose to step back, rethink and take in the information from our kids, ask for clarification, and sit down and discuss the information with them. We can turn these comments into a great learning opportunity for all of us.

Building a relationship for life

Jacqueline Kennedy Onassis might have said it best: *"If you bungle raising your children, I don't think whatever else you do well matters very much."* With that in mind, we need to learn from the Tonys of the world. We need to step back and rethink that his choice behaviors were an attempt on his part to control his Dad.

Even though his controlling choices carry with them some consequences, they did work. His choices were like flags and flares in the air that we need to pay attention to. These behaviors tell a story—a story of controlling versus a relationship.

This is where the issue of evaluating our relationship with our kids comes into play for us. Ask yourself: *"How do I want my kids to perceive me?* More importantly, *"How do my kids perceive me right now?"* Do they perceive you as caring, as concerned or involved? Or do they perceive you as cold, distant, controlling?

Ask your kids to tell you honestly how they perceive you in the areas we've covered so far. Do they perceive you as someone who reacts to problems, gets out of control easily, thinks, acts or feels stuck when problems arise, or takes on other people's problems, responsibility, decisions, power, control or choices?

Why am I asking you to do this? Because this is a way to sit down with your kids and share with them what you're learning in this book, and to show your willingness to become a great parent. Letting your kids know they're "raising you" as much as you're raising them will provide them with permission to share in the responsibility for growing up.

You'll find your kids will move toward you when they perceive you as someone they can have a relationship *with*. **Kids don't care how much you know until they know how much you care.** You're the head of the home. You're the one who defines, develops and designs the caring climate in the home. When kids were asked, *"What is it that makes a great parent?"* they always said it was a parent who encouraged, supported and trusted them, and made them feel like an important member of the family.

Now let's go on the other side and begin to evaluate your perceptions. How do you perceive your children? Do you perceive them as being fun, as caring, as hard workers—or as lazy, as rude, or as just one problem after another? If you perceive them negatively, how is that going to affect what you do toward them? Will this make you more of a controlling person, or less? Think about that.

Think of your own life as an adult. Isn't it true that if you know someone who's an excessive complainer, criticizer, or downright controller, you'll run for cover when you see them?

I rest my case, when I hear so many kids saying to me, *"You'd leave home too if you had a parent like mine,"* or *"The reason I shut down when my parents talk to me is that they don't talk—they always yell at me!"* *"My parents don't even listen to what I have to say."* *"My father always threatens me and I hate it."*

Rethink with me. Why do kids make these comments? Why do parents act like this? What's going on in this family? I hope at this point you're able to step back and rethink the answer to this question. I hope you'll be able to see that these problems are created by a "parent's choice" to react to problems, stay stuck on problems, focus on what they have no control over, think they have no choices, focus on controlling their kids' thoughts, actions or feelings, focus on wanting only what they want, focus on their kids as the problem, and look for their kids to change immediately.

I hope that just by reading this sentence you can actually feel the tension thinking like this creates! And what a setup for frustration!

Over the years, many kids have said to me, *"Why even try?"* *"My parents won't listen anyway."* *"There's no use even talking to them."* *"They're always screaming, fighting, and arguing."* *"Our house is so negative."* *"I hate going home, that's why I hang out with my friends so much."*

Our task as parents is to learn from these comments, to create an environment that will give our kids the motivation and permission to talk with us about anything they want. Our task is to evaluate our home environment and take an inventory of what makes us approachable. We can do this by asking our kids for help in evaluating the situation.

I want you to make a commitment that you'll work at developing ongoing rapport with each of your children. Before you can ever be effective as a parent, you must first spend quality time with your kids. This will take time and effort on your part—and don't give me the excuse that you don't have the time.

I've used the "I don't have time" excuse with losing weight. But when it comes right down to it, I have "the time" to watch three hours of television. I have "the time" to eat all the wrong foods, and I definitely have "the time" to whine about not having "the time."

No excuses! Schedule time for your kids. Find out what your children enjoy and spend time with them doing it. Start when they're young and go from there. The more actively you get involved with them, the better your relationship will be. Going to a movie requires very little activity. You sit, you watch, you stay quiet. Playing catch in the back yard requires activity, of which talking is usually a part.

Observe your children over the next few days and note the things they like to do. If they like building blocks, get down on the floor. If they like reading books, or playing with certain toys, hobbies or the like, get down to their level and get involved. If you want to build a relationship, take time to commit yourself to doing the things with your kids that they like to do.

Being on the lecture circuit could've kept me away from building a relationship with my kids, Christopher and Holly. I made a conscious effort to schedule my talks around my kids' lives. I saw a lot of speakers making a ton of money but with a collector's edition of wives and kids!

This wasn't for me. And I've seen the payoff for Carol and me in making this decision. We have two great kids you'd be happy to have your son or daughter hang around with or even marry! In fact, my wife and I have found our relationship with our kids just keeps getting better and better. Building your relationship with your kids over the years is like putting money in an investment account; the returns will definitely be well worth the investment you put in.

Here's what you can start doing to build a relationship with your kids:
- Make sure you spend quality time with them. Allow time for all of you to share your thoughts, your ideas, and your day.
- Watch your tone of voice, even when you're frustrated. You have total control over the raising or lowering of your voice.
- Spend time with them and let them know how much you love them. Tell them you like the special qualities they have (sense of humor, quick wit, ability to take care of themselves, responsibility, good thinking skills and the like).
- Demonstrate caring without demanding it in return. Demonstrate a sense of giving without getting in return.
- Teach and model what a good relationship is by building and improving your relationship skills with your spouse.
- Teach and model that saying "hello" first is within your control.
- Identify activities you all can share and enjoy.
- Create a special time to spend time alone with each child. Special time such as this creates an "I'm special" perception in your kid's mind.
- Get into your children's world and find out what they like to do.
- Remember that your children won't be with you forever, but that the thoughts about you and what you did or didn't do will always be with them.
- Teach and model that friendship starts with giving just to give, with little or no intention of getting something in return.
- Listen, listen, listen and listen, some more. When your kids come to you with a problem, don't immediately tell them what to do. Let them tell you what their problem is and allow them permission to talk about how they might try to solve it on their own first. Remember it's not by chance that God gave you two ears and one mouth!
- Allow your kids to teach you something they've learned. Kids love to

show off to their parents what they've learned in school, or what they've learned in a sport or a hobby they've taken up. Give them the opportunity to show you how they created something, what they learned in their sport or activity today, what they learned in school, what their thoughts and opinions are about what's going on in the world around them.

Home versus house—is there a difference?

Home	House
• Parent leads.	• Anybody leads.
• Expectations set by adults.	• No expectations set.
• Investment before return.	• Returns with no investment.
• Consistency and structure.	• Inconsistency, rigidity.
• Encourages choices.	• Takes over choices.
• Encourages self-control.	• Takes over control.
• Encourages decision making.	• Takes over decisions
• Encourages responsibility.	• Takes over responsibility.
• Tone of voice is modulated.	• Out of control tone of voice.
• Problems are opportunities.	• Problems viewed as crises.

Over time, the family has been the base of support where children get their basic needs met in life. But when we look at the family on the "new planet" and compare it to the family on the "old planet," we see more divorce, neglect, teenage pregnancy, drug abuse, single parents, and emotional and physical abuse than ever before. The family system is crumbling before our eyes, and the definition of family is changing just as rapidly.

Somehow we bought into the changing of that definition. We've been brainwashed into thinking this new system is normal. Think of all the people who want to argue with us today that divorce doesn't matter. It doesn't hurt kids. Fathers don't matter. They're not necessary. Day care is better than staying home with your kids.

We've been talked into believing we don't need a mother and a father to raise our kids, and that it's somehow okay to hand our kids over to strangers to raise them the majority of the day. But don't worry, we'll tuck them in at night, *if* we have time.

Just take a look at some of what's tearing the family unit apart today:
- The divorce rate is increasing. Think of the instability this brings into a child's life. Think of how this redefines the marriage vow, "for better or worse."
- After school latchkey programs for elementary kids are growing in numbers all across the country. On average, these kids aren't picked up until after 6 p.m. Most middle and high school kids are home alone, unsupervised until this time. No paid or unpaid help will ever have the commitment, investment and genuine love that you have.

- TV trays and the drive-up have made eating around a dinner table a thing of the past. Drive-up parenting might not be far behind!
- Prime time sitcoms are more and more sexually oriented in nature, making it more difficult for parents to teach the right way to behave before marriage.
- Children have less respect for authority figures, compared to days gone by. When this happens, children will get the message that respect doesn't matter.
- Children aren't as eager to learn the necessary academic skills and character assets in order to get ahead today.
- Many children aren't taught by their parents the value of doing their home work, because of the effort it takes on the parents' part to supervise it.

With these changes in mind, I want you to answer this question: What did *Ozzie and Harriet, Father Knows Best, The Donna Reed Show,* and *Leave It To Beaver* have in common? They were images of traditional two-parent families that emphasized sacrifices necessary to guarantee a cohesive family. They were willing to do the right thing when it came to raising kids of good character. They had a relationship with their kids, because the raising of their kids came first.

Here's what I think we learned from those shows about what a home should be:

- A place where you can go without fear, where you know you'll always be taken in, no matter what.
- A place where you can learn about responsibility, control and choices, to see which choices give you more responsibility and control over your own life, and which ones don't.
- A place where you learn to accept yourself for who you are and are given the space to do so.
- A place where you learn how to relate to others, and where you know there'll be a lot of extra hands and minds at your disposal to help.
- A place where you learn the true value of good character.
- A place where you learn to take control of your own life in preparation for eventually leaving home.
- A place you want to go to, where fun and humor abound.
- A place where your imagination can run wild and your dreams can be constantly examined.
- A place where the circle of life is openly discussed, from the joys of birth to grief over the loss of a loved one.
- A place where we're encouraged to express our emotions in appropriate and productive ways.

KEY POINTS TO REMEMBER

- If you choose to be a controller, you believe you can force others to behave the way you want them to. Good luck! Think about the prices you'll pay for controlling other people's thoughts, actions or feelings.
- The more we attempt to control other people, the more out of control we become.
- Punishment teaches a person what "not to do," instead of "what to do."
- Punishment teaches others that "someone" has more power, control and choices than they do.
- When punishment works, it unfortunately produces the "blowfish syndrome." It promotes thinking we have power over others, leading us further into the illusion of control.
- Parents will set themselves up for burnout when they want control over things, people or situations which they have no control over.
- What causes kids to move toward or away from parents is how kids perceive their parents. Their thoughts will direct their actions to move toward or away from parents.
- Create a home environment that provides: 1) permission to talk openly; 2) permission to demonstrate trust; 3) permission to share feelings; and 4) permission to demonstrate loyalty.

AREAS TO PRACTICE AND SHARE
Ask yourself two questions:
1. Am I doing this now?   **2. Am I going to start doing this?**

- Take time out of each and every day to just mingle with your kids.
- Make a plan to initiate a conversation with your kids each and every day.
- Make a commitment to give specific compliments to your kids, at least once a week, about either what they say, what they do, or how they look.
- Allow your kids the opportunity to demonstrate trust to you by allowing them to be involved in the choices they make each and every day.
- Say "I love you" each day to your kids.
- Make a plan to spend time alone with each child, doing something that requires both of you to be involved.
- Ask your kids to identify the ways you allow them:
    The opportunity to Talk?
    The opportunity to demonstrate Trustworthiness?
    The opportunity to express their Feelings?
    The opportunity to demonstrate their Loyalty?
- Sit down with your kids and discuss the ways in which your parents used to "discipline" you when you grew up. Discuss the pros and the cons of such discipline with them.
- Ask your kids about what makes you approachable and also unapproachable? Ask them to be specific, so you can make necessary changes to be a better parent.

Typical Problems...Dr. Mike's Practical Solutions

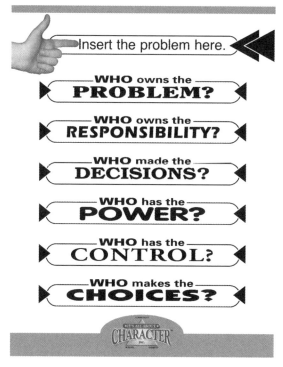

Insert the problem here.

WHO owns the
PROBLEM?

WHO owns the
RESPONSIBILITY?

WHO made the
DECISIONS?

WHO has the
POWER?

WHO has the
CONTROL?

WHO makes the
CHOICES?

CHARACTER

©Michael M. Thomson Ph.D. 1995

Pre-School/Elementary School

Typical Problem:

"My children are unruly around the house, and in public. I think spanking them is the best choice for controlling their behavior. Some people say spanking isn't right. I think it helped me keep my behavior under control when I was growing up. What do you think I should do here?"

Practical Solution:

Spanking will create one more problem, on top of whatever it is we're trying to solve. Spanking is done when "the parent" is frustrated with the child's behavior. I've never seen it fail that the parent is frustrated over situations or things they really have no control over. And because of thinking in an "out of control" fashion, the adult is usually taking on the child's problem, responsibility, decisions, power, control and choices and, unfortunately, believes spanking will teach the child something.

What spanking actually teaches kids is that someone with more power and control will step in and try to force them to behave in certain ways by inflicting physical punishment on them.

Let's face the facts: spanking is aggressive, hostile behavior. I hope you can understand that using aggression to deal with an aggressive child is not the best approach. To the child, it's humiliating, to say the least. Couple this with the act of aggression and you have a recipe for resentment from your child that will build with time. The best reason against the use of spanking is that research indicates it just doesn't work, and tends to make kids more aggressive and less well adjusted.

Sure you're going to be frustrated with your kids for their "poor choice" behavior. But remember; it's the behavior you don't like, it's not your child. Ask kids getting spanked if they feel the parent is doing it out of disapproval of the behavior, or of them? Most kids will say they feel their parents don't like them "at the time," and that's why they're getting spanked.

It's much better to talk to your child in a calm tone of voice. Use this as an opportunity for both of you to step back and rethink. Utilize *The Six Critical Questions*. Discuss the structure and expectations for behavior at home and in public.

Middle School

Typical Problem:

"I have a daughter who talks back and is belligerent. She just drives me nuts! How can I deal with this?"

Practical Solution:

Immediately step back and rethink. This is an opportunity for you to teach and model. Separate this problem into control, influence and no control, and you'll quickly understand that you can influence this situation based on what you have total control over, which is you. Remember you have total control over four areas in a relationship: demonstrating caring, asking questions, making statements, and providing alternative choices. The critical component of each of these areas is YOUR tone of voice.

If you keep humming, "I do jokes, I do windows, I don't do arguments," I think it will help you maintain your own sanity in this situation. You can see how easily it would be to react and take on the problem as well as the behavior in this situation. It's important for you to rethink and understand that some kids just like to be belligerent and talk back.

Unfortunately, they like this behavior because they know it works to get at you and others. It's just like one of those "lures" we talked about in the previous chapter, on Choices. Spit the lure out. Don't take on "their problem" or "their behavior." This is where you need to put this strategy we're discussing into overdrive and keep your focus on influencing them to make better choices.

You can work your way through *The Six Critical Questions* and see if you can figure out what's really bugging your daughter right now. If you can uncover the source of the problem that's causing this choice behavior, then you can ask her if she believes talking back and being belligerent will help solve the problem?

Ask her that, if she chooses to continue her behavior, will that choice cause her to lose out on some privileges that are important to her. This is where you can point out the structure in your home that when anyone has problems in life, which everybody does, you'll only talk them out, and not yell, scream or get out of control. Choosing to be belligerent and talking back won't solve problems, but will only create one more problem on top of whatever it is you're trying to solve.

High School

Typical Problem:

"My husband and I have very busy professional careers that have been getting more and more demanding over the past three years. Our son is really getting into a lot of trouble at school with bad grades, acting out behaviors and detentions. Recently he was arrested by the police for going into unlocked garages and stealing alcohol, along with other items. He's never been involved in this type of behavior in the past. How should I deal with him?"

Practical Solution:

The first thing is to let the school and law enforcement officials deal with your son the same way they'd deal with any other child who made these poor choices. Don't step in and protect your child from the natural consequences for such actions. Regardless of the underlying reasons, kids, like anyone, need to be held accountable for their poor choices made at the time.

This problem is an opportunity for you and your husband to step back, RETHINK and take an inventory of your RELATIONSHIP with your son. You've already identified part of the problem. You said you noticed a change in his behavior since you and your husband's professional careers became more demanding.

Your first question needs to be, *"Is my professional career more important than raising my child?"* If your answer is "yes," then take this book and any other book, audio or video on parenting and throw it in the trash. At least be honest enough to admit to others that *you* are the one who owns the problem, responsibility, decisions, power, control and choices for why your child is having trouble in his life right now.

But if you really want to influence him into making better choices from this point forward, then immediately think of these "acting out" behaviors as "flags or flares," indicating that he's in trouble in one or more internal psychological need areas.

From what you're telling me here, the poor choices your child is making are indicators (flags or flares) that he's unable to come right out and tell you what's really troubling him. I've become convinced over the years that some kids aren't always able to talk out what's going on with them at the time, but they sure display it in their poor choice actions. Be sure to step back and rethink, and read the signs your son is sending.

I've never seen it fail that kids who are in trouble and display behaviors such as these lack a solid RELATIONSHIP with their parents. When it comes to permission to talk, demonstrate trust, share feelings and demonstrate loyalty, these kids have always told me they don't feel as if they have this kind of relationship with either one or both of their parents.

This is something *you* have total control over changing. Once your kids see that you're willing to build a relationship with them, and that you're sincere, they'll begin to move closer to you. It won't happen overnight. But then, their behavior problems didn't happen overnight either.

Rethinking from "Wants" to NEEDS

UNDERSTANDING THE POWER of internal psychological needs as the motivating drive behind everything we think and do.

Look at the above drawing of a locomotive. On one side, the wheels are marked **SECURITY, FAITH, WORTH, and FREEDOM**. On the other side, they're marked **BELONGING, FUN, KNOWLEDGE, and HEALTH.**

These are the eight internal psychological needs that Dr. Gary Applegate introduced me to more than twenty years ago. They serve as the backdrop for this chapter. They're the driving force of the locomotive, just like they're the driving force of your life and the lives of your kids.

Now picture the wheels with spokes, which are identified as wants or pathways. Wants are different than needs. Think of wants as the spokes or pathways in a wheel that can lead to need fulfillment. These pathways can be either "good choices" or "poor choices."

I believe having numerous "good choice" spokes in a wheel will support the locomotive and keep it from bending or collapsing. The more efficient the pathways to need fulfillment (good choices), the more strength a person will have in the wheel. The more inefficient the pathways (poor choices), the weaker the wheel.

Wants are pathways to meet your needs. Wants are learned. Psychological needs are inherited. In the following list, determine which are wants or needs:

Going to the park, zoo or mall?
Making a team?
Getting a good grade?
Becoming a success?
Keeping a certain boyfriend/girlfriend?
Having a positive relationship with a parent?
Keeping a job?
Eating certain foods?
Using alcohol or other drugs?

Hopefully you can see that all these are wants, learned pathways to getting your needs met. Can you always get what you want? Can the park, zoo or mall be closed? Could you not make the team? Get a grade you don't like? End up feeling unsuccessful? Could a boyfriend/girlfriend break up with you? Could you lose regular contact with a parent due to a separation or divorce? Could you lose a job? Could you be told to avoid certain foods, alcohol or drugs, due to a health concern?

I want you to understand that these "wants" all start out with thoughts. They're mental pictures about what we want at the time. And since you've already learned that our thoughts direct our actions, could you "choose" actions like hoping, praying, talking, pleading, begging, demanding, trying to be nice, apologizing, or the like, all in an attempt to get what you want?

If these choices didn't work, could you then choose crying, anger, pouting, whining, depression, temper-tantrums, anxiety, and so forth, in an attempt to get what you want? And what happens when, even if you try everything, you still don't get what you want?

For example, you try hoping, praying or pleading with your parents to not get a divorce, and they don't change their mind. The answer's in another question. What was your initial intent with all of these choices? If it was to get your wants met, then you'll actually be setting yourself up for frustration, because you can't always get what you want.

So the real question here is: "What do you **really want**?" I believe that, if you step back and rethink, you'll begin to understand that the park, zoo, mall, making the team, getting a good grade, having a positive daily relationship with a parent, keeping a certain job, desiring certain foods, alcohol or other drugs are all just "wants" or pathways to meeting your internal psychological needs. In fact, they're all pathways chosen "at the time" that will meet your needs for security, faith, freedom, worth, belonging, fun, knowledge or health.

For example, if loss of regular contact with a parent through separation or divorce occurs, and you're choosing to think on a "want" level, how will you feel? Probably devastated. And if you were rethinking on a "need" level and this same situation occurs, how would you feel? Probably really sad.

Is there a difference between devastated and sad? If you had a choice between the two, would you rather be devastated or sad? Being sad is based on rethinking at a "need" level. And once you understand that your pathway for security, belonging and fun might not be met on a regular basis with a parent, could you choose to call a friend to either go to a movie, take a walk, play a board game, or go to dinner with?

Would these be "pathways" to put security, belonging and/or fun into your life? Would they be better choices than just sitting around with old "reaction" thoughts of waiting for one or both parents or the situation to change? Would they be better than old "reaction" choices like anger, depression, whining, pleading or the like?

We tend to think the problem is that we don't have our "wants" met. That's not the problem! As I said before, you can try everything, and you still might not get what you want.

This is where I want you to kick it into high gear and use the WHAT (*What's the problem?*), SO WHAT (*Is this a problem that's going to kill others or me?*), and particularly the NOW WHAT strategy (*What choices can I start making right now to move forward?*), and get off "the problem" and down to a need level as quickly as possible.

The problem is that we don't have our needs met efficiently. In fact, I believe there's only one problem we'll ever experience in life and that's when we don't have the efficient thinking or doing skills to meet one or more of our needs. That's why I think it's imperative to teach and model the efficient thinking and doing skills to our kids, so they understand that they might not always get their *wants* met, but can always get their *needs* met, if they choose to rethink.

Everything Is A Purposeful Choice

As difficult as it may seem for our kids and for us, we're not controlled by external events or people. We're motivated completely by forces inside us, and all our choices are our best attempt to control our own life.

I know it's easy to look to "out there" as what causes us to behave the way we do but, in order for our kids and us to go beyond where most people are, we'll need to give up our lifelong belief that what we do is a reaction or response to events around us.

It's not "out there" that we have total control over. It's our thoughts and actions! Teach and model this to your kids and they'll be way beyond where most people are.

So, what's the real reason why kids "choose to" pout, whine, cry, threaten, get depressed, drink, take drugs, skip school, wear strange-looking clothes, refuse to talk, give up, or run away? And why do some kids "choose to" fail, get in trouble with the school or the law, threaten suicide, succumb to peer pressure, or rebel?

On the other hand, why do some kids choose to do the opposite? The answer's in the following basic premise taught to me by Dr. Applegate:

"Everything we think and do is purposeful and is our best choice at the time to meet one or more of our internal psychological needs."

Up to this point, we've learned that behaviors like pouting, whining, crying, drinking, complaining, etc., are all choices people make "at the time" in their attempts to get what they want. And, as we've learned, just like a good fisherman, many of these choices are like "lures" from a tackle box.

Kids, like anyone, learn what "lures" to use to get what they "really want," which is to meet one or more of their internal psychological needs. If any of these choices work, they keep on using them until they realize they're not working, they begin paying prices in one or more need areas, or something or someone intervenes.

It's important for us to remember that, if uncorrected, these poor choices will lead to toddler, early childhood, adolescent and adulthood behaviors of concern. It becomes a vicious cycle.

What I want you to recognize is that purposeful choice behaviors like the ones listed above should send up a "flag or flare," alerting us to the fact that even behaviors like drinking, taking drugs, refusing to talk, wearing weird clothes, running away, threatening suicide, and various forms of rebelling are purposeful behaviors in meeting needs. People choose them because they work for them, "at the time."

Since we know these choices are learned pathways, we also know people can learn new ones at any time. The question that needs to be asked is: *If you continue with the choices you're currently making, which need areas might you pay prices in?* Nobody will ever consider making a behavioral change until this question is answered.

After observing this pattern of choice behavior in kids and adults for years now, I believe we all learned how to meet our needs with various behaviors right out of the womb.

If you want a great example of this, just watch a baby in a crib. While in the crib, kids become very creative with their choices in getting not only what they want but also what they "really want," which is having their psychological needs met. You'll see them go through a myriad of behaviors like crying, whimpering, and even banging on the crib rails.

All these behaviors are attempts to get them what they want, which is attention. All are attempts to get what they "really want," which is to meet one or more of their internal psychological needs, like belonging, worth and security.

Kids learn quickly that all these choices can be used successfully in pulling their parents toward them and satisfying their needs. Just like tiny little fishermen, they learn very quickly which lures work best to help them get what they want.

My wife Carol and I were "hooked" with a lot of choice behaviors by Christopher and Holly. When I think back to those days, I swear they knew exactly which behaviors to pull out of their tackle box in order to get not only what they wanted, but what they "really wanted" from us. And did those "choices" on their part work?

Ask our kids and they'd probably both say, *"Wonderfully well!"* What I've also observed over the years is that the longer any person goes on using choices like crying, pouting, whining, drinking, complaining, etc., without intervention from parents or others, the more they'll continue to use these behaviors later in life. As I stated earlier, if you're catching fish with these "lures," why change the lure?

All Behaviors Tell A Story

Okay, maybe this is starting to make sense to you when it comes to these types of "choice behaviors," but some of you might be thinking, *"What about the more serious and harmful behaviors?"* What helped me better understand the behavioral "lures" of refusing to talk, wearing weird clothes, angry outbursts and/or violent behavior, running away, threatening suicide, and various forms of rebelling, and their connection to psychological needs, was to step back and rethink that these choices are like flares in the air or flags waving.

To me these "choice behaviors" are really telling a story of either what's going on or what's not going on in a particular situation. It helped me rethink that these behaviors are really pathways to meeting internal psychological needs. I began viewing them as choices that were saying, *"Notice me; this is the best choice I know of at the time to meet one or more of my needs."*

It helped me to better understand these "poor choice" behaviors were like a flare in the sky or a flag waving, indicating that this person is most likely frustrated in one or more internal psychological need areas. Knowing this allowed me to step back, rethink and play detective in order to figure out what it was they "wanted" at the time, and equate that to what they "really wanted," which was to meet one or more of their needs. I could then effectively use *The Eight Areas of The Power of Productive Choices* and *The Six Critical Questions* as my backdrop in teaching them better choices to meet their needs.

From this point forward, I want you to consider "poor choices" as just that, poor choices made at the time. Don't jump to the conclusion most "reacting" people do, and assume the person making them is a "bad" person. These choices made at the time are telling a story. They're saying *"Hey, notice me, I'm making choices that are meeting one or more of my needs. To you they might appear as not to be the best of choices but they do meet my needs at the time."*

You might be thinking, *"Why don't they just tell us they're frustrated?"* Oh, but they are telling us. Their "chosen" behavior at the time doesn't lie. For many, they can't come right out and tell us, due to the controlling people or circumstances around them. For others, they simply don't know how.

At this point in their lives, I believe many haven't been taught the rethinking skills we're talking about. So they use what they've seen others use to meet their needs. Does it work? Sure it does. Tony, the boy from a previous chapter, who wore the 666 on his knuckles, wrote "Hail Satan" on his notebook, wore what looked like forty pounds of earrings on one ear, and shaved one side of his head, was also telling a story of the frustration in his life. He was shooting off flares and waving flags like there was no tomorrow.

Once I started to rethink that his choice behaviors were really telling a story, I was able to understand that he was making his "best choices he knew of at the time" in his attempts to deal with the controlling behavior of his father. His choices were also the best choices he could think of at the time to meet his psychological need of worth (through controlling and powering.)

The problem is that with choices like these, he'll pay prices in need areas such as belonging (some people will be turned off by his style of dress), worth (he'll actually lose a sense of power and control), and freedom (his choices will get his parents actually more on his back instead of off his back).

The typical response by most parents to poor choice behavior by their kids is to jump in and try to stop it. A typical parent would probably REACT to any of these behaviors by getting into an argument that would include screaming, yelling, threatening and other forms of controlling behaviors, all in an attempt to bring about change.

Reacting to poor choice behavior isn't the answer. Stepping back, rethinking and looking behind the behavior for the answer is.

By doing this, you'll begin to understand that:

- Most people are focused on getting their "wants" met at the time. They need our help to aid them in rethinking what the problem really is.
- All behaviors are purposeful and are a person's best attempt "at the time" to meet one or more internal psychological needs. These individuals need our help to learn alternative choices they have total control over in order to meet those needs.
- The "flags" or "flares" people send up in the form of their "poor choice" behaviors indicate they're frustrated in one or more of their need areas. As a parent, this is your opportunity to step back, rethink and:

A. EVALUATE YOURSELF FIRST in two areas:

1. **Your RELATIONSHIP.** Ask yourself three very important questions; *"Are the choices I'm making and the kind of person I am right now pulling my kids toward me or pushing them away from me?" "How do I want my kids to perceive me in each of the eight psychological need areas?"* and *"How do my kids perceive me right now in each of the eight psychological need areas?"*

2. **Your HOME ENVIRONMENT.** Ask yourself the following questions in each of the eight internal psychological need areas:
SECURITY *(Do you teach your kids that true security in life is in having good thinking and doing skills in order to take effective control of the daily problems of living?)*
FAITH *(Do you provide an opportunity for your kids to believe not only in themselves but also in a power greater than themselves?)*
WORTH *(Do you allow your kids to demonstrate that they can take on their own problems, responsibility, decisions, power, control and choices?)*
FREEDOM *(Do you allow your kids to demonstrate that they can make good choices even when you're not watching?)*
BELONGING *(Do you teach your kids the importance of their intent when starting, building and maintaining healthy relationships?)*
FUN *(Do you teach your kids to enjoy life?)*
KNOWLEDGE *(Do you teach your kids the value of seeking out and acquiring a constant stream of new information in their life?)*
HEALTH *(Do you teach your kids the thinking and doing skills to take care of their physical and psychological health?)*

B. EVALUATE YOUR KIDS' BEHAVIOR OF CONCERN by asking:

1. *"What **NEED AREAS** might your kids' "poor choice" behavior be meeting at the time? What **NEED AREAS** might they pay prices in with these poor choices?"*
2. *"What possible influence might **FRIENDS, SIGNIFICANT OTHERS, THE HOME, SCHOOL OR COMMUNITY ENVIRONMENT** have on your kids as it pertains to the problem at hand?"*

C. BRAINSTORM ALTERNATIVE CHOICES that can be provided to your kids in order to help them deal effectively with the frustration they're experiencing. Help them stop trying to just get their "wants" met and begin brainstorming new choices they have total control over in getting their "needs" met.

D. BRAINSTORM POSSIBLE INTERVENTION STEPS that might be necessary in order to influence your kid's "poor choice" behavior. If the behavior you're concerned about doesn't change or is more serious in nature, you'll need to step in and take control of their choices. *Can you accomplish this intervention alone or do you need to involve others?* Involving outside help is *not* a sign of weakness. It can actually be a sign of strength on your part as well as an indication to your kids that you're willing to go to the next level if their "poor choice" behavior doesn't change.

Meeting your needs with your kids versus through your kids

When your kids feel a sense of need fulfillment and a relationship with you, they're going to be generally happy, and major behavior or discipline problems will be rare. Sure, there'll be the ups and downs of everyday life, but serious problems between you and your kids are less likely if they feel there's a sense of need fulfillment when you're in their life.

Let me emphasize a very important point, so you keep remembering it: **If *you* choose to meet your needs *through* your kids, then you'll be setting yourself up for frustration whenever your kids don't think, act or feel the way you want them to.** And this is *not* the way to think if you want to save your sanity!

The more *you* want your kids to be doctors, lawyers, dentists, married, parents, successful, rich, etc., the more you'll push them to achieve these goals for *you* in order to get "your needs" met. Here's the key point: nothing we do will alienate children more than to be forced to be something they don't want to be.

If you decide your relationship with your kids "is your life" or "is your identity," I want you to ask yourself a very important question: *"Who's really running your life?"* I want you to also follow this up with two more important questions *"How does giving yourself, your identity and your need fulfill-*

ment over to another person put you in a weak position?" "What prices do you pay for being overly dependent on someone else for your need fulfillment?"

Now, don't just read these questions and move on. Answer them! Don't choose to think you can't live without your kids, no matter what happens. As tough as it sounds, you always have the ability to take effective control of your own life, regardless of the circumstances that might come up. When your kids are either ready to leave home and live on their own or, God forbid, if something happens to them, **YOU** always have control over meeting your own needs, regardless of the circumstances.

I don't want this to sound morbid, but it's a very secure feeling for me to know that if something were to happen to my wife or me, my kids realize life will go on. I feel secure knowing they have the skills to live productive and fulfilling lives. As a family, we've all been subtly aware over the years that we've learned how to meet our needs *with* each other and not *through* each other excessively.

Rethinking in this way will help you teach and model to your children what they can do every day in all their environments to meet all their needs—in spite of whatever should come up in their lives. Help them understand that they may not always get what they want, which will create some frustration, but that their psychological needs can always be fulfilled if they choose to look at alternative choices to meet those needs.

Keep humming to them that **"you're never stuck unless you think, act or feel stuck."** By doing this, you'll focus on rethinking and not reacting, by turning problems into opportunities, and by focusing on the choices you have total control over. I'm really convinced that if you teach your kids the skills to meet their needs in all their environments, you'll be the winner in the long run. And your kids will perceive you as a teacher, rather than a problem solver when problems arise.

Near the end of each of the previous chapters, we've included an "areas to practice and share" section. What follows at this point are the thinking and doing skills in each need area that I suggest you "practice and share" with your kids.

AREAS TO PRACTICE AND SHARE

Ask yourself two questions:
1. Am I doing this now?   *2. Am I going to start doing this?*

Security: *"I feel secure when I know I have the skills to deal with the daily problems of living. I also feel secure in knowing I have the personal power and the control over my own life, and I realize I can't control what anyone else does or thinks."*

What you can do to teach and model *Security:*

- Teach and model that true security is based on having the efficient thinking and doing skills to take control of your life. It's also knowing you have the ability to continue building new skills on a daily basis.
- Teach and model that true security is not in material possessions, which you always have a chance of losing. True security is in having good thinking and doing skills. Nothing "out there" can ever take away your personal skills.
- Teach and model that life is a series of everyday lessons called problems. Problems are opportunities—opportunities to evaluate what choices you made worked and what didn't work. You either learn the lessons or repeat the poor choices and accompanying problems.
- Teach and model that we don't have to depend on other people for problem resolution or need fulfillment. We have the power, control and choice to take on the responsibility of learning the skills to solve our own problems and meet our own needs.
- Have your kids identify people their age who are great role models in each of the eight internal psychological need areas. *Ask why they'd name them as role models? What good choices do these people make that makes them great role models? Now ask your kids who do they think would name them? Why? Why not?*
- Let your kids know that, in life, you may not always be able to get what you want, but if you step back and rethink, you can always get your needs met. What you want may not be in your control, but meeting your needs in alternative ways is always in your control.

*Faith: "I feel a sense of faith in my life when I have a positive **belief** in myself and also in a power greater than myself. It's this belief that creates a positive attitude in myself, and in life in general."*

What you can do to teach and model *Faith:*

- Teach and model that you can celebrate the positive in yourself, others, situations, things, and a power greater than yourself, regardless of what happens in life.
- Teach and model accepting and letting go, even if there's no reason.
- Teach and model a love for nature and the universe.
- Adopt the concept of WHAT (*What's the problem?*) SO WHAT (*Is this a problem that's going to kill me, or others?*) and NOW WHAT (*What choices can I start making right now to move forward?*)
- Teach and model that in most cases, and regardless of what problems come up in life, you'll always be able to get through them.
- Teach and model an awareness of things people didn't create.
- Teach and model an awareness of what's positive in a person's physical, intellectual and emotional makeup.

Worth: *"I feel a sense of worth when I know I'm in control of **achieving**, each and every day. I know I'm capable of going beyond where I was yesterday, through my thinking and my actions."*

What you can do to teach and model *Worth*:
- Teach and model that a true sense of Worth comes from inside yourself and not from other people, things or "out there."
- Teach and model that external sources of Worth may feel good in the short run, but with time will fade.
- Teach and model that a true sense of power and control will be felt when using *The Eight Areas of The Power of Productive Choices* and *The Six Critical Questions* in everyday situations. And, when problems arise, give them some guidance as they work their way through, using these tools.
- Allow your kids the opportunity to demonstrate responsibility and a feeling of power over their own lives by formulating their own decisions. You can be there to guide them but allow them to go through and even struggle with the decision-making process on their own.
- Share the positive with your kids regarding what they say and do; catch them making good choices, particularly when they thought no one was watching.
- Help your kids step back and reflect on where their life has been, where it is now, and in what direction they want it to go in the future. Encourage your kids to take risks and look for opportunities to achieve and go beyond where they now are.

Freedom: *"I feel a sense of freedom in knowing I have the power and control over the **choices** I make in my life. Knowing I can choose to rethink rather than react to events in my life provides an incredible sense of freedom."*

What you can do to teach and model *Freedom*:
- Teach and model to your kids that they're responsible for all their own personal choices in all situations, regardless of what goes on around them.
- Teach and model to your kids that the environment, other people, and "out there" does in fact influence them, but that's as far as it goes. The environment, other people and "out there" do not have the ultimate control over their thoughts, actions or feelings. They do.
- Allow your kids to develop responsibility, power and control in their own life by letting them handle their own problems by themselves. Do what you have to do to control yourself from stepping in.
- Allow your kids to have a say in refining your expectations regarding their behavior at home, at school or elsewhere. Explain if need be why you expect certain behaviors from them in these areas. Reach a mutually agreeable decision regarding the unshakeable-unbreakable "line in the

sand" point where, if they cross that line, you'll step in and take control of their life and their choices if need be.

- Challenge your kids whenever you hear them attempting to place blame on others for their own poor choices. Help them identify that "others" only influence the ultimate choices they themselves have total control over.
- Teach and model to your kids that how they choose to think directs how they ultimately choose to act and feel.
- Teach and model to your kids the benefit of changing what they have control over, instead of spending energy on people, things, or situations they have little or no control over.
- Teach and model to your kids that the use of negative language such as "have to," "must," "can't," "should," "forced," "addicted," "if only "out there" would change," "I can't stand it," and so on, places them in a "choosing to be stuck" position. Help them see the benefit in quickly looking for what "can be" done through the choices one makes.
- Create a list of behaviors like complaining, anger, whining, drinking, taking drugs, etc. Have your kids determine: 1) which need(s) these choices meet; 2) which need(s) these choices will create frustration in; and 3) better choices that could meet their needs.
- Violent behavior, drinking, drugs, attempted suicide, anorexia or bulimia are serious "poor choices," as well as "flags and flares" many people send up in an attempt to alert others that they're frustrated in one or more of their internal psychological need areas. Help your kids to step back, rethink and identify which psychological needs can be affected when people choose these behaviors. Help them brainstorm how using *The Six Critical Questions* along with *The Eight Areas of The Power of Productive Choices* could help these people live differently.
- Review with your kids the list of the eight internal psychological need areas. Ask them to be honest with you and help you evaluate your strengths and your weaknesses in each of the need areas.

Belonging: *"I feel a sense of caring when I have friends who care about me and when I care about others in my life. The beginning of a relationship starts with intent. **Give to give** without expecting something in return."*

What you can do to teach and model *Belonging*:
- The amount of time you spend with your kids is not the key to a great relationship. Make sure you spend quality time with your kids. Make a plan to really get involved in what they like to do. Your investment in building a relationship with them will provide an incredible return.
- Monitor your tone of voice, which is directly related to how much you want what you want in any given situation. Teach your kids that the tone of voice will continue to rise when people are trying to get something or

someone to change in areas they have little or no control over.

- Spend time with your kids and let them know how much you love them. Tell them what it is about the special qualities they have (i.e. sense of humor, quick wit, ability to take care of themselves, responsibility, and good thinking skills).
- Help your kids see the value in demonstrating caring without demanding it in return. Show them they can give to others without getting something in return.
- Teach and model that the most important step in beginning a friendship is your intent. If your intent is to just be friendly, with little or no intention of getting something in return, you'll be in control. If your intent is in having the other person accept you, like you or be your friend, you're putting yourself in an out-of-control position.
- Listen, listen, listen and listen some more.

*Fun: "I feel a sense of fun in my life when I'm laughing, experiencing excitement, humor or a general good time. Knowing **I can make fun happen** is the key to having fun in my life."*

What you can do to teach and model *Fun:*
- Brainstorm a list of the inexpensive fun activities you can do as a family.
- Plan to have some type of fun with your kids every day.
- Teach and model the value of looking at the humorous side of problems. Ninety-eight percent of all problems won't kill anyone.
- Sit back and just watch your kids. Identify what they like to do for fun. Find ways to involve yourself in their fun activities.
- If you think *old*, you'll act *old* and ultimately feel *old*. Let yourself go and become childlike. Smile just to smile. Laugh just to laugh. Look for fun and enjoyment whenever and wherever you can.
- Play board games with your kids. Teach and model how you can choose to play board games simply for fun and togetherness, rather than having to win or even compete.

*Knowledge: "I feel a sense of knowledge when I know that the **more information** I put into my life, the more alternatives I have for meeting more of my needs."*

What you can do to teach and model *Knowledge:*
- Instead of just saying, *"Why in the world would people even make those kinds of choices?"* encourage your kids to look at the strange as familiar and the familiar as strange. Accepting that the world is filled with individual choices helps your kids become more tolerant of other people making the choices they wish to make.

- Turn off the car radio when driving with your kids. This gives you both a chance for talking and sharing.
- Read the newspaper, watch the news, or listen to the radio and share something you learned with your kids. Teach them that keeping up with the everyday news is a great way to put more information into their lives. The more information they have, the more power they'll have.
- Teach and model to your kids the importance of brainstorming alternative choices when frustrated. Help them understand that evaluating what they're currently thinking and doing will open up new alternative choices for them.
- Teach and model to your kids that putting new information into their lives gives them power, only if they use it efficiently. Not all learned information can be used in constructive ways. Help your kids understand that some information can be learned, thought about and challenged, BUT if acted out can create problems.
- Encourage a regular and never ending evaluation of each of the eight psychological need areas. Take each need area and really evaluate the choices being made by you and your kids. From this evaluation, determine the need areas you all need to work on.
- Use the hub of a wheel as a visual aid, with the spokes representing the pathways people choose to satisfy those needs. Help them step back and identify the pathways in which you all meet each of your needs. Get into a discussion and determine with each other if the pathways are "good choices" or "poor choices."

Health: *"I feel a sense of health in my life when I know there's **balance** between my physical and psychological needs."*

What you can do to teach and model *Health:*
- Think about your body from head to toe. Discuss the importance of them taking control over their personal hygiene. For instance, discuss the importance of brushing their teeth, washing their hands and face, bathing on a regular basis, taking care of their hair, the use of deodorants, make-up, perfumes, etc. Identify with them the benefits when taking control of these areas and what they lose if they neglect them.
- High blood pressure. Obesity. Sleeplessness. Fatigue. Rethink every health problem as really an opportunity to learn new thinking and doing skills. Take some time to discuss with your kids that many health-related problems are due to multiple poor choices that are really within the person's control over changing.
- Teach and model that learning about how your body works is really something people don't focus on until parts of it break down. Knowing you have a heart is one thing. Knowing what choices people make to develop either a healthy or unhealthy heart is another thing. You can have

some great discussions with your kids on parts of the body rarely talked about.

- *"Junk food is so irresistible. I know it's fattening but I can't control myself. I know I need to lose weight, but I just don't have the time."* Teach and model that people have total control over what foods they choose to put in their mouth. And as to the excuse of not having time, you have "time" to eat! Choose wisely.
- Teach and model that the use of tobacco, alcohol or other drugs is always going to be a choice. For instance, when it comes to drinking alcohol, you have a great opportunity to discuss the difference between abstinence, drinking and getting drunk. It also gives you the opportunity to discuss your expectations regarding those substances.
- Teach and model the benefits of physical fitness. Provide opportunities for exercise as a family. This doesn't have to be a major undertaking. Just taking a walk, doing yard work, or playing active games with your kids, is better than choosing to be a couch potato or watch others making these active choices.

KEY POINTS TO REMEMBER

- Wants are pathways to meet your internal psychological needs. Wants are learned.
- Psychological needs are inherited.
- Psychological needs are dual purpose. They can motivate and they can frustrate.
- We're motivated completely by forces inside us, and all our choices are our best attempt to control our own life.
- People will never consider making different choices until they believe the choices they're currently making aren't helping them enough to get their psychological needs met.
- All behaviors are purposeful and are a person's best attempts at the time to meet one or more internal psychological needs.
- All behaviors tell a story. Begin to perceive "poor choices" and negative behaviors as flares or flags that indicate a loss of need fulfillment in one or more areas.
- Frustration results not only from not getting what you want, but more importantly, from not getting what you "really want," which is to get your internal psychological needs met.
- Most people are focused on getting their "wants" met at the time. We all know we can't always get what we want. But if we choose to step back and rethink, we can always get our needs met. Our kids need our help to aid them in rethinking what alternative choices they can make to still meet their needs, even if their wants or pathways are blocked.
- We should view poor choices or misbehavior by our kids as a flag or

flare, alerting us to the probability of frustration in one or more of their need areas.

- Once we see that frustration, we need to look at teaching and reinforcing the learning of *The Six Critical Questions,* and *The Eight Areas of The Power of Productive Choices.*
- Rethink that some "poor choices" and behaviors our kids might use are like fishing lures, to hook parents and other people into meeting their psychological needs. We can either spit the lure out or swallow it and take on their problems, responsibility, decisions, power, control and choices. Spit the lure out!
- The choices you use to meet your needs may be either efficient or inefficient. The critical difference is that with efficient choices, you don't have any prices to pay in other need areas.
- If your kids perceive you as need fulfilling, they will move toward you and cooperate more. If you're perceived as need reducing, they'll move away from you and be less cooperative.
- If *you* choose to meet your needs *through* your kids, then you'll be setting yourself up for frustration whenever they don't think, act or feel the way *you* want them to.
- We can empower ourselves by changing our thinking from "what people want" to "what people really want," which is to meet their internal psychological needs.

Typical Problems...Dr. Mike's Practical Solutions

©Michael M. Thomson Ph.D. 1995

Pre-School/Elementary

Typical Problem:

"My child came home crying and told me one of the neighborhood kids was being mean to her by hitting her and pushing her around. This has happened on numerous occasions. I didn't see it, but it gets me really upset that kids are like this nowadays. What should I do?

Practical Solution:

When we find our kids being picked on, we tend to react like a mother bear protecting her cubs. I want you to step back and rethink this problem. Help your daughter calm down and ask her about what happened. Play detective and get as much information as possible. If she owns all or part of the problem, help her see her part in it. If you determine she doesn't own any part of the problem, it will lead you to the next step.

Share what you've learned with the parent(s) of the other child. Before you do, be aware that your attempt will be to just "influence" them and not change them or their child.

Even if you think sharing this will be "in their best interest," you might get the opposite of what you expect. If so, tell the parent that the child isn't welcome to play with your daughter unless there's a change in attitude.

Be sure to help your child stop focusing just on the problem (the mean neighborhood kid), and get down to the concept of needs. Help her understand that this kid's behavior upsets both of you in the need areas of security, fun, and belonging, etc. Knowing this allows both of you to step back, rethink and understand that this "mean neighborhood kid" represents only one pathway to the fulfillment of those need areas.

If you both stay stuck on just trying to get your "wants" met (this kid or the parents acknowledging that change in behavior is needed) then you'll both stay frustrated for quite some time. This is the time to kick in high gear with the WHAT (*What's the problem?*), SO WHAT (*Is this a problem that is going to kill me or others?*), and particularly the NOW WHAT strategy (*What choices can I start making right now to move forward?*).

Understanding you can't always get what you want will help you get off the problem and begin looking for ways for both of you to get your needs met. And even if the relationship with the other kid ends, life will go on. And the same is true for the parents who refuse to acknowledge any wrongdoing by their child. Life will go on for everyone. And so will the fulfillment of your needs, as long as you continue to step back, rethink and focus on building other pathways to meet those needs.

Middle/High School

Typical Problem:

"My son comes from a really dysfunctional home. His father, who has never really been in the picture, is an alcoholic. My son has also just completed a drug treatment program for his own addiction. I'm really trying to help him create a better life. I feel like I'm to blame for what's happened. What can I do?"

Practical Solution:

I don't want you to get into the "victimhood/blamehood" mentality. Yes, it sounds like your son's had a rough time. But you're not to blame for anyone taking alcohol or other drugs. Period, end of sentence. These were choices his father and he made at the time to deal with whatever they "wanted" and, to be more specific, what they "really wanted," which was to meet one or more of their internal psychological needs.

Regardless of the circumstances, I want you to focus on what you can do now to influence your son in meeting his needs in more efficient ways. Alcohol and other drugs are the most "efficient" of the inefficient choices people make, quickly blotting out the difference between what they want and what they have. Alcohol and other drugs are very need fulfilling "at the time."

The problem is that the use of these substances creates a loss in other needs areas. A few of the areas might be belonging (people move away from you when you're intoxicated); fun (you're not a lot of fun to be around when you're throwing up, and the like); and security (you feel secure with the drugs in you but insecure when they're not).

Knowing this puts us in a great position to look at various ways to help your child begin to start building new pathways into his life to meet the needs that at one time were satisfied by drugs.

Some people find need fulfillment by joining various recovery support groups. These groups do work, because, for the most part, they're need fulfilling. But remember, these only take up a certain amount of time. You might hear them say, "So what am I going to do the other 23 hours of the day?"

This is where you need to teach them *The Eight Areas of The Power of Productive Choices,* and *The Six Critical Questions.* By influencing them with what you're learning in this book, you'll help them obtain more skills that can be used in satisfying these once frustrated needs.

Make a plan to sit and discuss the suggested pathways for need fulfillment in each need area within this chapter. Make a plan to put into your home environment and your personal relationship at least one of these suggested areas, so that life will be focused on the future and not the past.

Rethinking from "External" to INTERNAL

UNLEASHING THE INCREDIBLE POWER WITHIN. There is no stopping you when you learn this.

I choose:
To live by choice, not by chance;
To make changes, not excuses;
To be motivated, not manipulated;
To be useful, not used;
To excel; not compete;
To choose self-esteem, not self-pity;
I choose to listen to the inner voice, not the random opinions of others.
Anonymous

"YOU have the power, the control and the choice to make either good choices or poor choices; it will always be your choice." I remember years ago standing up on stage and telling people in the audience this very powerful statement. At that moment, I knew I'd begun to see the world differently. I felt I really had the edge on what gives people true happiness and productivity in their lives. And it was at that moment that I knew I had total control over my own happiness and could now teach this to other people.

After many years of listening to people's problems as a therapist in private practice, and to numerous callers to radio or television talk shows I was a guest on, I learned that true happiness occurs when people truly believe they have total control over their own lives and the choices they make. You could see it in their eyes and hear it in their voices that, regardless of the "external" out-there events or people, they knew they had the "internal" power and control to make their lives better.

As a therapist, I'd often put myself in an out-of-control position. I believed that if you (client) tell me your troubles; I'll be an external problem-solver. You tell me your problems; and we'll both end up wearing Don Ho shirts, strumming ukuleles and singing, "Feelings, Whoa, Whoa, Feelings," until the cows come home!

My education, training and colleagues groomed me to work with people in this way. It created the thinking that I (the powerful therapist and wizard) will find solutions to YOUR problems and, hopefully, we'll both feel good. Right? Wrong!

My thinking as a parent was similar. I was educated and trained that when my kids have problems, I'll step in and be the almighty wizard and parental problem solver.

It's like playing the role of the apparently all-knowing, all seeing, almighty wizard in the classic movie, *The Wizard of Oz*. Yet, in the end, we saw him behind the curtain pulling levers, turning wheels and pushing buttons in order to create the "external" illusion of almighty power and control.

Hopefully, you realize by this point that I don't want you to go there. YOU ARE NOT the "external" source of power and control to take on or solve your children's problems, responsibility, or decisions. I truly believe that as a parent your power and control will come once you begin to realize how people (including yourself) choose to set themselves up for more frustration when their happiness is dependent on something or someone "out there."

This is no different than what Dorothy, the scarecrow, the tin man and the lion found out. They learned that the Wizard really wasn't going to solve their problems for them, and that what they always wanted was really inside them all the time. The Wizard, in his wonderful way, taught them the true meaning of security when he told them to look inside themselves for the "internal" answers to their individual problems.

The Wizard also taught them that they had no control over anyone or anything "out there," and that **the solution for a better life and happiness comes from how they deal with the world, and not how the world deals with them.**

Think about it: *As a parent, can we always get our kids to do what we want? Do we have control over everything they think or do? Do we really have total control over getting them to be more responsible, cheerful, affectionate, or less demanding?* Trying to take control of any of these is like trying to stop a raging flood. Good luck! And think about how much energy people use in trying to control these external "out there" events in their lives. I get pooped just thinking about it!

"How can I ever get ahead in life when I'm the child of a left handed vegetarian?"

The dumbing down of our society

The "psychologizing" of our society is alive and well! On the old planet, misbehavior was viewed as right and wrong, acceptable and unacceptable, permitted and not permitted. Period, end of sentence.

Enter the psycho-babbling stream of shrinks, talk show hosts and armchair psychologists around us today. Misbehavior is either the result of low self-esteem, a brain snafu, food allergies, being the child of a left-handed vegetarian, or some other gene-dysfunctional problem (see cartoon above).

This type of thinking supports the "I'm not responsible for my choices" mentality. It's the classic victimhood/blamehood mentality. It's the "external" forces beyond my control line of nonsense that has driven me right to the edge over the years. Hogwash! Each person has INTERNAL free will. We're not mysteriously driven by some power beyond our control. We're not the victim who's able to point to "out there" as the reason for how we think, act or feel the way we do.

Think about this; it's so easy for many people to blame guns, the Internet, violent videos, movies and games for kids' violence today or even their change in morals. Most of these "influences" would be virtually powerless in the face of involved, intact, family units with parents praying, eating, talking, playing and just being with their kids.

There are always going to be influences coming from "out there." That should be a wake-up call and our cue to step in and teach what's right and what's wrong. We have a responsibility to teach our kids that these "external influences" are just examples of the variety of choices in the buffet of life.

And just like the power of free speech via these forms of entertainment in today's society, we always have the power of choice. And so do our kids.

This is no different than allowing anything or anybody to get in the way of applying yourself to your goals. "Out there" becomes just an excuse. No one can victimize you or control you UNLESS you let them! *You* must be the one who gives them permission. No person or thing has power over you, unless you think they do.

Saying someone or something "out there" victimized or controlled you isn't being self-responsible. Success and failure in life are the outcomes of your own choices and behavior. That is what personal responsibility is all about. Failure at something is only a lesson, a stepping stone to our next choice in accomplishing our goal. We've all failed at something; it's a part of life. It's our "wake-up-call" to get a grip, get a life, and get going!

You respected me!

Two sisters from the Orlando, Florida area shared with me a great story of the impact of my material on their lives. They went to dinner at their father's house one night. They were so excited about what they'd been learning through my seminars, books, audiocassettes and videos, and wanted to share their excitement with their father.

Near the end of the dinner, they began sharing with him highlights of *The Eight Areas of The Power of Productive Choices* and *The Six Critical Questions,* and how they were using them with their two kids.

Their father stopped them mid-story and said in a loud and stern voice, *"I don't like this power, control, choices idea. That's the problem with parents today. I don't know who this Dr. Mike guy is, but I just want you two to know that when you grew up in my house, you RESPECTED me. I don't want to hear anymore about this power, control and choices stuff!"*

The sisters went on to tell me that their father is the type who'll never change his mind on something, and that even trying to discuss change was just wasting energy. The best part of the story was when the sisters told me that, as they left that night, they looked at each other and said, *"it wasn't respect, it was FEAR!"*

They went on to say it was the "external" fear and "controlling" that their father had over them that worked, not respect. They were afraid of him. And fear, as we've learned, didn't teach them how to take effective control of their own lives. It taught them that "someone or something" outside of themselves had more power, control and choices. It also created one more problem in their lives.

That is why I want you to step back, rethink, and teach and model to your kids that the people who feel terrific in life are the ones who know they have the INTERNAL skills to get what they want. They're the ones who believe in themselves—who achieve, because they risk something every day. They're always going beyond where they were yesterday. They know they have the power, the control and the choices to make their lives what they want to make them.

Unfortunately, so many of us have been conditioned to believe that, if we can just find some "outside" stimulus to motivate others, that doing this is the key to somehow magically get kids to think, act or feel the way we want them to. As I've previously said, the discipline approach grew out of this belief system. This and other controlling approaches have fostered a wrong belief that "someone or something" has more power, control and choice than the person with the problem behavior has.

We need to teach and model the "internal" skills incorporated in *The Eight Areas of The Power of Productive Choices* and *The Six Critical Questions* that your kids need to learn at any age to become productive people in today's society. This will be in spite and despite what is either going on or not going on around them.

Sticks and stones...

"How come you never?"
"Shut up!"
"Where were you when the brains were passed out?"
"You never listen."
"You're so lazy."
"You're such a pig."
"Why can't you ever...?"
"Is that the best you can do?"
"You've been one problem after another all your life."
"I'll never trust you again."
"You'll never amount to anything in life."
"You are so stupid. How stupid can you get?"
"You'll be the death of me yet."
"Don't you have any sense at all?"
"Nothing's ever good enough for you."
"I can talk to you until I'm blue in the face and it never does any good."
"Can't you do anything right?"
"Can't you get it through your thick head?"
"When will you ever learn?"

Now, I don't know about you but these "external" messages would affect anybody. I've had people tell me to "just let it roll off your back like water off a duck's back." Well guess what...I'm not a duck!

Years ago I was trained by one of the best in the psychology field, the founder of Reality Therapy, Dr. William Glasser. In his lectures, Dr. Glasser stated many times that *"Children find in the eyes of their parents the mirrors in which they define themselves within the relationship. Fill them with noth-ing, they become nothing. They have a tremendous ability to live down to the lowest expectations in any environment."*

If you set low expectations, they'll set their sights at that level. If you set high or reasonable expectations, they'll strive for those. The choice is yours. When they hear negative messages at home, kids' feelings and actions are bound to be negatively influenced. Children learn to program themselves from the messages they receive from others.

Children aren't born with attitudes about themselves. They enter the world clean and fresh, without any preconceived notions of the world around them. They're hungry for information. Their attitudes about themselves develop from the experiences they have, including the messages they receive from parents and others. The attitudes they develop about others and events in the world come from what they receive in the form of messages from us.

Who has control over those messages? Who has control over providing information to them? We do. Go back and look over the list of statements again. **These statements are made only when *we* are frustrated with our kids about something *we* aren't getting.**

Everything you do or say to your kids, intentionally or not, will have an effect on them. It will affect their thinking about themselves, about the world around them, including you; it will affect how they choose to act, and it will obviously affect their feelings about themselves and the world around them. If you really want to be a better parent, then evaluate what messages "you choose" to influence your kids with. *Did messages like the above affect your thoughts, actions and feelings when you were growing up?*

How about changing some of our messages and sending these to our kids:
"I love you."
"You're a winner."
"Just let me know if I can help."
"The sky's the limit for you."
"You're going somewhere in life"
"Whatever the problem, you'll be able to handle it."
"You're really making responsible decisions for yourself."
"You must feel really good about the choices you're making."
"You're not a bad kid; you're just making poor choices."
"You really take care of yourself."
"We can always count on you."
"You really are a pleasure to be around."
"I love it when you're so positive about everything."
"It's great to hear you singing around the house."
"I can tell you're going to be very successful in life."
"Always remember that whatever you choose to do in life is your choice."
"It's great having a son/daughter like you."
"You're the best."

Earl Nightingale said, *"We become what we think about most of the time."* With that in mind, what's your best guess as to what your kids think about most of the time? Are their thoughts positive or negative? And what kind of thoughts do they have when it comes to you? How about when it comes to their home environment? When it comes to their future? Or maybe even when it comes to life in general?

If you don't know the answers, then sit down with your kids and begin to ask these questions. Evaluating what we do to set up our home environment is our first step in creating a better relationship with our children. It's an area we have total control over. We need to look at ourselves first before we look to our kids for change. Sure, kids have areas that need to change also, but why wait for them to change? Why spend so much energy in trying to change them?

Start with yourself first. Start by evaluating yourself and what you say or do to create a positive or a negative environment. Jesus said it quite well in Luke: *"Don't worry about the speck of sawdust in your brother's eye until you take the plank out of you own."* Who are we to judge others and their behaviors until we look inside ourselves first? That's why I stress the use of *The Six Critical Questions* to use in our own lives FIRST. After all, you grow by correcting your own behavior, not by correcting others.

Building an internal fire

You've already learned that you're going to pay prices for trying to motivate your kids through coercion, threats or fear; but you can influence them with what you choose to do. You can teach your kids that they're in charge of their attitude, which is always something they have control over adjusting.

You know your kids are a work in progress. They're on a pathway toward adulthood. They need you for guidance. They need you to teach them how to deal with the daily problems of living. To abdicate being their anchor, weathervane and moral compass is like throwing them in the middle of the ocean and saying "Good luck." It's a recipe for disaster. You'll get the most influence with your kids not by lighting a fire beneath them, but by building an "internal" fire WITHIN them.

Here are some of the "internal" fires you can build:
- All family members are responsible for their own thoughts, actions and feelings, and have the ability to make good choices or poor choices. The bottom line is that it's their choice to make either one. There's no reliance on others to rid them of "their own problems."
- Your attitude is everything. It will determine the quality of your life. WHAT YOU FOCUS ON IS THE DIRECTION YOU'LL GO. Focus on your problems and they'll become bigger everyday and lead you in a direction you won't be happy with. Rethinking and focusing on solutions

and choices you have one hundred percent control over will lead you in a different direction. The problems will begin to fade away.

- Live in the present. It makes no sense to focus on the past. There's no changing the past or, for that matter, predicting the future. That's why they call yesterday history, tomorrow the future, and today as a gift, a mystery and an opportunity.
- You're never stuck unless you choose to think, act or feel stuck. There's no sense in choosing to sit back and focus just on problems. The focus should be on solving problems. There are three choices whenever you feel stuck:
  1. Give up and stay stuck with the problem.
  2. Make negative choices that will create even more problems.
  3. RETHINK, make positive choices you have full control over and move forward in life.
- Create a positive success-focused environment wherever you are. Many times in our lives, we may think our choices at the time really stink. But the bottom line is that we still have choices. Choosing to not do anything is a choice. Not choosing is easier than changing. It takes no effort. It's just a watered down version of "I give up."
- When you hear "I give up" or "I don't have to" you know that anybody can choose to give up and not do anything. That will always be a choice. The question is: *"How will choosing to do nothing help you get what you want in life?"*
- Don't fall into the famous "Yeah, but" trap. Everything after the word "but" is an excuse why we "choose" not to make the right choice. "But" I was busy, I don't have the time, I forgot, it's too hard, and other like statements, keep us from taking control over our own lives.

The two-minute theory

Take a look at the following list of potential problems children may be faced with growing up:

- Someone is being mean to them
- A parental separation or divorce
- Not being picked for an activity
- Getting a bad grade
- Getting grounded or put to bed
- Getting a speeding ticket
- Getting fired from a job
- Friends turning on them

As you read these, you can get a sense how some kids and their parents might choose to "react," focus on the "problem," become "out of control," and feel they have "no choices" available to them.

I want you to go beyond where most people are, and "teach and model" to your kids that the "external" world will always influence their thoughts, actions and feelings BUT…that's all the "external" world can do. Teach and model to them the "Two-Minute Theory" when it comes to the above list, as well as any "external" problems or events they experience from "out there."

What I mean by the "Two-Minute Theory" is to spend approximately two minutes at the feelings level regarding these problems—BUT THAT'S IT!

I believe that if you choose to go beyond that point, you'll be reinforcing to your kids that they're in fact depressed, angry, miserable—and that it's BECAUSE "out there" is the CAUSE. Don't go there! Let you kids know you agree that when someone's mean to them, when parents separate or divorce, when they get bad grades, grounded, put to bed early, a speeding ticket, fired, or when friends turn on them, it does in fact create a negative feeling.

BUT, beyond just expressing their "feelings" about the "external" person, situation or event for more than two minutes, they're not depressed, angry, or miserable anymore. They're now making the same "INTERNAL" choices people make when they're frustrated.

This is where you need to kick it into high gear. This is where you need to teach and model to your kids that ninety-eight percent of people or situations WILL NOT KILL THEM. Frustrate them, yes. Kill them, no! "The only people without problems are dead," "The world is filled with jerks," and, "In a tornado, even a turkey can fly" all come into play here.

Like it or not, the problems and the jerks they're experiencing are a part of life. But the best part is that, with *The Eight Areas of The Power of Productive Choices* and *The Six Critical Questions,* they can fly, just like a turkey in a tornado!

Sure, you and your kids will have feelings about the problems, but you now know you CAN CHOOSE TO RETHINK, turn problems into OPPORTUNITIES, focus on the CHOICES you have CONTROL over, keep building better RELATIONSHIP skills, increase your pathways for NEED fulfillment, continue to believe you have the INTERNAL skills to deal with all these situations in life, and understand and accept that these are all situations we can break down into PROCESS steps we have control over.

Now I know some of you reading this are saying, "Well, this is easier said than done!" You're absolutely right! It takes very little effort to react, focus on the problem, become out of control, feel you have no choices, get into controlling behavior, focus on getting your wants met, focus on "out there" as the problem, and wanting the solution or outcome to a problem to occur right now.

If you or your kids want to go that way, call me, write me or e-mail me, and let me know how life is going. I'll bet you dollars to doughnuts that you or your kids won't be happy campers. To which I'll say politely: "Happiness: It's Your Choice."

KEY POINTS TO REMEMBER

- You have the power, the control and the choice to make either good choices or poor choices; it will always be your choice.

- Regardless of the "external" influences in life, you have total control over your thoughts, actions and ultimate feelings.
- The solution for a better life and happiness comes from how you deal with the world and not how the world deals with you.
- All of us have internal free will. We have the power of choice.
- In the majority of cases in life, nothing outside yourself can victimize or control you unless you allow it.
- Success as well as failure in life are the outcomes of your own choices and your own behavior.
- Kids learn to program themselves from the messages they receive from us as parents.
- True security is having good rethinking skills to deal with the daily problems of living.
- You'll get the most influence from your kids, not by lighting a fire beneath them, but by building an "internal" fire within them.
- Teach your kids the "Two-Minute Theory" when they come upon situations, people or events that frustrate them.
- You're never stuck unless you choose to think, act or feel stuck.
- Everything after the word "but" is an excuse why we "choose" not to make the right choice.

AREAS TO PRACTICE AND SHARE

Ask yourself two questions:
1. Am I doing this now?   2. Am I going to start doing this?

- Sit down with your kids and share with one another the last time you "reacted" negatively to a situation, a person or an event. Take each area you identify and brainstorm what better choices you could have made if you'd chosen to step back and rethink using *The Eight Areas of The Power of Productive Choices* and *The Six Critical Questions.*
- Discuss with your kids the concept of peer pressure. Ask them if they know of people who use peer pressure as a great excuse in blaming "out there" for the poor choices they themselves have made.
- Discuss the issue of trust with your kids. Ask them to decide on whether trust in them is based on the choices you make as a parent, or the choices they demonstrate as a son or daughter. Once trust is lost, discuss how long it might take to gain it back.
- Brainstorm with your kids all the situations you've seen in the last twenty-four hours where a person could have benefited from using the Two-Minute theory.
- Discuss with your kids the statement: "The solution for a better life and happiness comes from how you deal with the world and not how the

world deals with you." Do they agree with this statement? Do they disagree with it? Why or why not?

Typical Problems…Dr. Mike's Practical Solutions

Insert the problem here.

WHO owns the
PROBLEM?

WHO owns the
RESPONSIBILITY?

WHO made the
DECISIONS?

WHO has the
POWER?

WHO has the
CONTROL?

WHO makes the
CHOICES?

©Michael M. Thomson Ph.D. 1995

Pre-School/Elementary

Typical Problem:

"My upper elementary child received a drop in a letter grade on a recent assignment. The reason the teacher gave was that she didn't follow directions by putting her name on the paper, even though she finished the assignment. She's also been given a detention by this teacher when she's not in her seat when the bell rings. My child is really smart but is getting very frustrated with this teacher. What should I do?"

Practical Solution:

Well, maybe your child is smart academically, but is failing in the behavioral category. If she's as smart as you say, she should have figured it out that the problem is not "external" via the teacher and his expectations. The problem is that she's not following the structure set down by this teacher.

You need to teach her that, in order to make it through life, she needs to make the right choices. Since the problem here isn't academics, you as a parent need to help your child step back, RETHINK and look on this as a behavioral problem.

It's a problem she has the POWER, CONTROL and RESPONSIBILITY over when it comes to the DECISIONS being made. You need to get her off the teacher as the "external" source of the problem. The teacher, like others she may meet in life, will just set the structure and will state what the expectations are. This is the moment when the choice to make good choices and poor choices comes over to your kids.

Middle School/High School

Typical Problem:
"I'm really angry about the movie and music industry today, for throwing things at our kids that are making them more disrespectful, obnoxious, aggressive and, in some cases, more violent. What if anything can I do as a parent to influence this?"

Practical Solution:
The information kids are exposed to via television, movies, music and even the Internet does have an influence on them. But that's it—influence and not control. The influence these industries have on our kids can be both positive and negative depending on how we process the information and what we do with it.

I don't want you as a parent to "react" to this potential problem, causing you to then focus on the industries (out there) as the problem. This is your cue to step in with both feet. The television, stereo, radio and computer are inanimate objects that require electricity and most likely cable fees in order to come into your home.

YOU have the POWER, CONTROL and RESPONSIBILITY to monitor these CHOICES. Not your kids. And not the television, movie, music or computer industries. When something you don't agree with comes your kids' way, YOU can turn the television, computer, stereo, radio or computer off. The First National Bank of Mom and Dad that funds these items can be closed in an instant.

You can set the structure of what, when and how these options will be allowed in your child's life, your home, your car, and so forth. You don't have to "react" and blame the industry that's creating this. The industry has the freedom of speech under the constitution.

You have the power of choice under your roof. You can also step back, RETHINK and look at it not as a problem but as a teaching OPPORTUNITY for you and your kids.

Vulgar language, sex, drugs, lying, cheating, stealing, violence, or a myriad of poor choices that can come up via these industries can actually be

OPPORTUNITIES for some really great discussion between you and your kids. Freedom of speech, via the television, movie, music and computer industry in a free society, provides a wealth of opportunities to discuss the pros and cons of such choices.

The bottom line is that your kids need to learn from YOU how these entertainment industries work, so they can begin to make decisions in their own lives that are reflective of not only your structure and your family values, but also that of society's values.

You have a great OPPORTUNITY to teach that choosing to think, act or feel like some people do in these industries may bring with it consequences. You need to help your kids understand that people who CHOOSE to think, act or feel this way will pay prices for their behavior at some point in life. Explain to your kids that life is similar to a buffet at a restaurant, with lots of CHOICES available, but not every CHOICE the best one for them.

Unfortunately, some kids won't have the emotional support, guidance or teaching of caring parents. Some will have lazy and irresponsible parents, who won't take the time to provide a buffer between these industries and their kids.

In my experience, these parents will point the finger of blame at the industries as the problem, failing to recognize that they have three fingers on that hand pointing back to them. And is that the industries' PROBLEM and RESPONSIBILITY, or the parents?

Rethinking from "Outcome" to PROCESS

JUST BABY STEPS! Why you must learn how to tie it all together for massive success

Sometimes it seems like the whole world is designed toward the future instead of focusing on living today. Waiting for that driver's license, waiting to graduate, waiting until you're eighteen, waiting until you're twenty-one, waiting for that bartender to ask for that I.D., waiting for the weekend, waiting for vacation, waiting for marriage, waiting for retirement, and so on and so on.

Even if it's just watching the clock at work, counting the minutes until quitting time, you're choosing to give up the enjoyment that takes place between the start and the end of the work day. The problem here is that we're not into the *process* of life, but into the *outcome* of life. We're **"waiting"** for a future event that will somehow make us feel better. Yuck!

It's also no news flash that we live in a quick-fix society that wants everything solved by noon tomorrow, at the latest. We want results now. We don't want to wait. We want our eggs cooked now, our meals zapped in an instant, our phone calls to get through right now. We watch as the whole world of televised fantasy gives us the impression that problems can be solved quickly.

Computers are in a race for the fastest processing time, microwaves strive to be the fastest, and if you have a headache, don't take 400 milligrams, take 800 milligrams of extra strength, buffered, super-charged aspirin. The list goes on and on. Television ads tell us a certain shampoo, deodorant, toothpaste or soap will make us happier, healthier, sexier, and of course, more popular.

If all these implied promises were true, fights, arguments and divorce courts would be extinct by now. You and I both know that just thinking about or waiting for the "outcomes" in life will lead us actually to more frustration, because these outcomes aren't always in our total control.

"When I get the kids through high school," "When I put the last kid through college," "When I get the mortgage paid off," "When I finally get to retire." Surely you know of some parents who can't wait until their kids go to college, so they can get some peace and quiet around the house. And you've probably often heard friends talking about how much they're looking forward to the day they retire.

It seems everyone has these checkpoints they've set up for themselves, where their lives are supposed to be better once these events occur. Sooner or later, we must realize these are all things we have no control over. They're out of our control. They're in the future. We have influence over them, but in order to save our sanity, we need to step back, rethink and focus on the "process" steps we have complete control over to get to these outcomes.

Now don't get me wrong, there's nothing wrong in looking toward the future, in planning goals and activities. But if the future dominates your thinking, if you believe happiness is only in the future, you're choosing to put yourself in a stuck position, waiting for a future "outcome" that may never come.

What I've learned as a parent

I've learned:
- That my kids and I are works in process.
- That what I do will make a difference in my kids' lives.
- That the only people without problems are dead!
- That the world is filled with jerks. I can learn from every one of them how not to think, act or feel.
- That in a tornado, even a turkey can fly! I will never give up.
- That I can learn the skills to meet my internal psychological needs in all environments.
- That "out there" will only influence me. I have the power of choice.
- That it's a lot easier to react than to step back and rethink.
- That we have the power, control and choice to do the right thing, even when no one's watching.
- That anything outside of yourself is not true security.
- That two people can look at the exact same thing and see something totally different.
- That you're never ever stuck unless you choose to think, act or feel stuck.
- That your attitude is everything.
- That I'll be judged by my last worst act.
- That every day is an opportunity for me to improve my life.
- That winning really isn't everything. There's no real victory without honor.

- That it can take years to build up my character and only seconds to destroy it.
- That "It's All About Character," and that my character really does count.

Rethinking as a process parent

As I've stated in many of the preceding chapters, we as parents are actually set up for frustration with our kids, by indirectly and sometimes directly being told by "out there" that "we" should have control over our kids, their behavior and accompanying problems.

Think about what a setup this is. *We* are expected to quickly come up with "the answer" that's supposed to solve our kids' problems. Get *them* to behave. Get *them* better grades. Get *them* to do their homework. Get *them* to change their attitude. And the list goes on and on. These are all expected behavioral outcomes we're supposed to be in total control of. Think again!

As you're already aware, using *The Eight Areas of The Power of Productive Choices* and *The Six Critical Questions* has launched me to a new planet! I hope that by reading this book you're on your way there also. Wanting our kids to behave, to get better grades, to do their homework, to change their attitude, and so on, are all wants that relate to the concept of "outcome." And if you and I are trying to just get our wants met, good luck!

We've already seen that you can't always get what you want. But if you're into "process" thinking, your focus is on building new pathways in order to meet your internal psychological needs. Sure, it would be magical if we could just snap our fingers, or say a secret word like one of those hypnotists do up on stage, and have our kids do what we say, but we know better than that.

You now know you can look at these "problems" in a whole new way. You can break any problem you or your kids will have into the PROCESS steps needed to solve them. You now know you can teach and model to your kids that "you're never stuck unless you choose to think, act or feel stuck."

As a result of this new way of thinking, you can now RETHINK about the problem, look at it as an OPPORTUNITY, focus on the areas you have one hundred percent CONTROL over, and identify the CHOICES needed to get there. Just by doing these simple steps, you're teaching and modeling to your kids that they can learn the INTERNAL skills to meet all their NEEDS in all their environments. This is very empowering.

There's an old saying that relates to the concept of outcome to process. It states: *"I came to therapy hoping to receive butter for the bread of life. Instead I emerged with a pail of sour milk, a churn and instructions on how to use them."* Giving each of our kids the skills you've been learning in order to deal with the daily problems in life is what PROCESS is all about.

Giving them butter for the bread of life is what OUTCOME is all about. It requires no effort on your kids' part. It's *you* solving *their* problems. It teaches them nothing about the power, control and choices they have to take effective control of their own lives. Using a PROCESS way of rethinking, you're helping your kids know they're going to experience a lot of sour milk (problems) along the road of life.

But if they learn the rethinking skills we're talking about, they'll quickly learn they have the power, control and choice to turn all problems into opportunities. Knowing they're *"never stuck,"* that *"the only people without problems are dead,"* that *"the world is filled with jerks,"* and that, *"In a tornado, even a turkey can fly,"* helps them to step back and rethink all problem situations they'll come in contact with.

PROCESS thinkers know they have 1440 minutes of each day to either react or RETHINK. The best part is that in most situations you have total control over how you choose to think, act or feel.

Don't forget what we learned back in the Rethinking chapter. Most problems you and your kids will experience probably won't kill you or them. You'll need to react and focus on the outcome only about two percent of the time. That's when there's a choice of your children hurting themselves or hurting someone else. The rest of the time, you can help them focus on the process "baby steps" needed to solve the problem at hand.

How long will it take?

Many parents want "instant productivity, instant relationship, instant trust, or to become the instant parent of the year." Hey, who wouldn't want that! But that's not what *The Power of Productive Choices* process is all about. What you're learning and what you should practice and share is a rethinking system that takes time to implement, not only in your own life as a parent but also in the flow of everyday life. Any book, training program or technique that promises "free, instant, and easy" results is probably not based on correct thinking.

How long will it take to build a productive family? How long will it take to implement what you're learning in this book? It will take as long as it takes. What? That's right! It will take as long as it will take. Most people don't want to hear this, but you're starting to understand it because you know relationships (like the ones with your kids) are always in the process of change.

A relationship grows from day to day without end. That's why pre-school has its own set of problems, and the same is true for elementary, middle and high schools, and beyond. It never ends. That's what "process" is all about.

Here's an exercise I use in my seminars. Picture having a key in your hand, the one that opens the door to your office. And once that key opens the door, you can relax, right? Well, maybe.

I want you to rethink with me and hold that key in your hand, put it in the door and, *if* it opens, say to yourself, *"Well, I guess I'm working here today!"*

You see, I don't know if you're going to be working there tomorrow, next week or next year. The company could lay you off, go bankrupt or, worse yet, could fire you. But if you're a PROCESS thinker, you'll understand that *if* the door doesn't open you're not stuck.

You're never stuck unless you choose to feel stuck. The problem of the door not opening just presents you with an OPPORTUNITY to RETHINK, focus on the CHOICES you have CONTROL over, look for the INTERNAL solutions to the problem at hand, and understand that happiness is not only getting what you want in life but is also being in the PROCESS of getting what you want.

If you have good skills, you can always get another job. Sure, it'll be frustrating, but you can't control the "what if" situations in life. What you can control is how you choose to think about each and every situation you encounter.

It isn't difficult to become a process-oriented parent or even teach this to your kids. By rethinking that each day is a new OPPORTUNITY to solve problems will help you and your kids rethink in a PROCESS fashion. It really helps me to remember that there are 1440 minutes in each day. With so many minutes available I can "choose" to focus on my next choices that will move me along through the day in a positive and productive manner.

This should also help your kids. Problems, as we've been learning, are inevitable. You can choose to be unhappy or to be happy. It's your choice. We've been encouraging you repeatedly to teach and model that it's not "out there" that creates happiness or unhappiness.

You have kids. You will have problems. As parents, we need to help our kids break their problems down into small steps they have control over achieving. For example, think of the specific steps required to reach the outcome of hitting a ball with a bat. Hitting the ball is the outcome. All the specific steps that get to that point are part of the PROCESS. Just telling a kid to hit the ball is why most kids who don't hit it get frustrated. Telling them over and over to just hit the ball, keep your eye on the ball, and the like, are actually frustrating the situation and not solving it.

What I've found that helps me rethink about the process steps that go into hitting a ball is to think of myself as having to teach someone from another planet the specific steps involved. This person has no clue what this activity is all about, and has never heard about it or seen it.

You might start with pictures, or watch a person hitting a ball. Next, you might break down the specific steps involved. If you had a videotape, you could freeze-frame each step. These are all the steps the batter has control over. You might explain how to swing a bat, how to hold the head, feet, upper and lower part of the body, the arms, etc. As you can see, there are many, many PROCESS steps to hitting a ball.

With this example in mind, can you see how easy it is for you and your kids to just focus on the OUTCOMES in life? If you do, you'll be setting yourself and them up for frustration.

Take a look at the following list:

- Getting a good grade
- Making an athletic team
- Graduating from school
- Making more money
- Getting a job
- Making a new friend

You can almost feel the frustration people might experience if they choose to focus on the OUTCOME of getting a good grade, making the team, graduating, making money, getting the job, or making a new friend. "What if" they run into obstacles, meet someone they don't get along with, and so on?

If you were into PROCESS, you would be surprised if these didn't happen! If you're into PROCESS, you just keep using each of the RETHINKING skills noted in this book. Regardless of whether you get the outcome you want or not, you know you're focused on what you have one hundred percent CONTROL over 1440 minutes of every day.

Will I really make a difference?

Here's a great story that may help you and your kids with thinking in a PROCESS fashion.

As the old man walked the beach at dawn, he noticed a young man ahead of him picking up starfish and throwing them back into the ocean.

Finally catching up with the youth, he asked him why he was doing this.

The youth responded, "The stranded starfish would die if left until the morning sun."

"But the beach goes on for miles and there are thousands of starfish. How can your effort make any difference?"

The young man looked at the starfish in his hand and threw it back to the safety of the water.

"It makes a difference to this one," he said.
Anonymous

How many negative people like the old man in this story are you going to be approached by? How many are going to tell you you won't be able to make a difference? We change the world and ourselves one starfish at a time. What we do does make a difference with our kids. Teaching our kids that what they do in life can make a difference is important for us to keep in mind. Their choices count. Their character counts.

The real question in this story is: how long will this young man continue to pick up starfish? I believe the answer is he'll do it as long as *he* sees the "internal" value in doing so as just the "baby steps" he needs to take in order to accomplish his goal.

Parents, just like the young man, will continue to hang in there through thick and thin, *if* they choose to look at problems experienced along the way as part of the process of parenting. Like starfish, your kids will wash up on the shore from time to time. And, as a PROCESS oriented parent, you'll pick them up, brush them off, get a little teaching in if you can, and throw them back.

There's no OUTCOME to parenting. After all, the only outcome in life is death! Parents will experience many problems in their journey through parenthood. Making a decision to tackle those problems with the aid of *The Eight Areas of The Power of Productive Choices* and *The Six Critical Questions* is what we're suggesting. Like the story above, it will be one starfish at a time. Or, in the parents' eyes, it will be one problem at a time.

Even though you'll experience problems with your kids, the benefits of parenthood are there. But where? Where are the benefits at the moment? That's the problem sometime for all of us as parents. We want to see the results of our parenting. We want to see the payoff for what we've done, in the behavior of our kids.

The problem is that it will take time to see the benefits. Our hard work and perseverance will pay off. Your teaching and modeling of *The Eight Areas of The Power of Productive Choices* and *The Six Critical Questions* will eventually take hold. Maybe not by noon tomorrow, but it will take hold.

Just like the person picking up the starfish, patience becomes the word of the day for parents. There'll be times when others will tell you to get tougher, pull more privileges, yell more, threaten more, discipline more, and so on. Some might even tell you to give up, that you'll never make a difference! But you now know that using the material in this book is just like the young man walking on the beach and saying, *"It makes a difference to this one."* Go make a difference with the ones you love.

To set goals or to not set goals?

We've all been taught to have goals in our lives. That's an okay concept, as long as we break those goals down into PROCESS "baby steps" we have control over. Otherwise, we'll be setting ourselves and our kids up for frustration.

Many times, when we or our kids are confronted with a problem, the solution can seem overwhelming. Here are some steps an old friend of mine, Dr. Gary Applegate, author of *Happiness: It's Your Choice*, taught me to follow in achieving goals. I think they'll help you and your kids make more effective plans that are:

Simple:
Small and uncomplicated, not self-defeating.

Specific:
Focused on specifically what you'll do, when, where and how you'll do it.

Rethinking:
A rethinking plan that's focused on changing the way you look at your problems and the way you look at the world around you.

Repetitive
Something you can work on each day or repeat often, in order to make it a new habit in your life. Avoid the "one-shot deal" quick fix method.

Independent:
Contingent or dependent upon you alone and not upon others.

Immediate:
Put your plan into action immediately; the longer you delay, the less likely you'll put it into action.

Written:
Put it in writing and refer to it daily. Let others know the changes you're making. Put your plan for change on the refrigerator, bedroom wall, bathroom mirror or elsewhere, where you can refer to it often.

Skill Building:
Develop skills that will take you one step beyond where you are now. Most change requires time. "One choice at a time" or "One step at a time" might be your motto here. It takes time to learn and apply the information in this book. Remember, it took all your life to get where you are today. Take it slowly. Enjoy the thought that you are making changes, one step at a time.

Creating plans with the above steps in mind will help you achieve, go beyond where you are today, build self-confidence, and become a risk taker. The next time you or your kids fall short of a goal, step back and match your steps up with the eight steps above. If you're like me, you'll find you're not using several of those guidelines.

KEY POINTS TO REMEMBER

- Life is a process; the only outcome is death.
- Living your life in a process fashion is looking at meeting as many of your needs as possible in each of your daily environments. Need fulfill-

ment doesn't depend on your location, but on your willingness to look for ways to build new pathways to meet your needs.

- When creating goals, break them down into process steps you have control over.
- Make your plans simple, specific, repetitive and immediate.
- Make your plans independent of other people or things.
- Write your plans down and refer to them often.
- Make your plan skill-building, by including the productive thinking areas.
- When it comes to making any changes in life, many people have lots of excuses for not following through with their plan for change. You have 1440 minutes of each day to make the right choices.
- Life is not a cakewalk! There's no growing without going through some pain.
- Your self-esteem and sense of inner power come from suffering through life's painful moments.
- Keep reminding yourself that most of life's problems are going to be frustrating, but probably aren't going to kill you. They're really opportunities to practice what you're learning in this book.
- Two percent of the time, you *will* need to "react" to a situation at hand. Many people have these figures backward, and pay significant prices for "reacting" versus "rethinking" problem situations.

AREAS TO PRACTICE AND SHARE

Ask yourself two questions:
1. Am I doing this now?   2. Am I going to start doing this?

- Look for opportunities to teach your kids process thinking and doing skills. Take a situation like being stuck in an airport due to a delayed flight. Brainstorm pathways your kids could choose to use, in order to meet their needs while waiting. Discuss the importance of breaking a problem situation like this down into process steps to meeting your needs, versus staying stuck on trying to get your "wants" met, such as a flight that's not going to go out on time.
- Take a situation like wanting to get a better grade. Brainstorm with your kids all the individual steps that go into the higher probability of getting a better grade. Take each of those steps and evaluate them according to the eight steps to good plan making.
- Take each one of the eight steps to good plan making and discuss with your kids the benefit in using that step in making effective plans:

Simple	**Independent**
Specific	**Immediate**
Rethinking	**Written**
Repetitive	**Skill Building**

Typical Problems…Dr. Mike's Practical Solutions

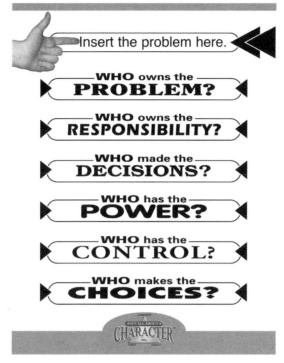

Insert the problem here.

WHO owns the
PROBLEM?

WHO owns the
RESPONSIBILITY?

WHO made the
DECISIONS?

WHO has the
POWER?

WHO has the
CONTROL?

WHO makes the
CHOICES?

CHARACTER

©Michael M. Thomson Ph.D. 1995

Pre-School/Elementary School

Typical Problem:

"There are so many issues in children's lives that a parent needs to be concerned about as they're growing up. I want my kids to develop good character. Sometimes I feel they want me in their lives and sometimes I feel they don't. How do I know when to step in and when to back off?"

Practical Solution:

They needed you when they were younger. You were there with the wet nap, the tissues, the bottle and the pacifier. You taught them to ride their bike, brush their teeth, comb their hair, pick out their clothes, and to say "please" and "thank you."

As they get older, one minute they're sweet and lovable, the next minute sour and unmanageable. They're more sophisticated than to throw themselves on the floor in a temper tantrum, but their whining and complaining skills have hit an all-time high.

Kids need people to look up to. Their prime role model is you. You can't influence your kids to be honest if you're not. You can't teach them to be good citizens if you don't do your part. You can't teach them to make good decisions and be responsible, if you're always doing things for them. You can't teach caring and fairness, if you lose your cool and get all bent out of shape. There's nothing worse than someone who tells us to do something and then does just the opposite.

The big question for us is: *"Where are we, regarding these areas of character?"* Are we good role models of trustworthiness? Honesty? Respect? Responsibility? Fairness? Caring? Citizenship?

We all want our kids to be successful in life. I believe it's not the person with the most money or material possessions who wins but the person with the most skills. When deciding to step in or not, ask yourself *"Would I want the decision I'm about to make to appear on the front page of the newspaper?"* *"Would it hurt or enhance my reputation?"* *"Is stepping in right now the right thing to do?"* You don't have to react to everything. Don't sweat the small stuff. In fact, most of it will be small stuff.

Pick your battles and where your lines are going to be drawn. A "no tobacco, alcohol or other drug use" stance is an example of an unshakeable, unbreakable structure in your home. Even though you'll probably hear the "everybody is doing it" song, stand by your structure.

Disagreements over hair, makeup, curfew, friends, music, food, activity involvement, and the like are typical. The key is to make your points, set your structure, and let your kids own the problem, responsibility, decisions, power and control and choice. You'll discover that allowing your kids the opportunity to discuss why they want what they want gives them the feeling that, at the very least, you're listening to them.

Middle School

Typical Problem:

"How do I motivate an unmotivated child? He's always saying "I give up," "It's too hard," "Why even try?" How do I get him to be a productive person?

Practical Solution:

First of all, step back, and RETHINK. Focus your thoughts on this being an OPPORTUNITY for you to focus on what you have complete control over in this problem. You'll quickly recognize that you have complete control over demonstrating caring, asking questions, making statements, and providing alternative choices.

The toughest thing to do here is to not react by "motivating" your child through various negative means. Focus on building a RELATIONSHIP, first through your tone of voice, and then through your demonstration of caring. Identify what you see in his behavior and ask for his help in identifying where he sees himself in life right now, and where he wants to go.

Remember, your tone of voice is critical. Raise your voice and you're dead in the water! Help him understand that when people CHOOSE to use words like, *"I give up," "It's too hard," "Why even try?"* it's because he's frustrated and sees the solution to a problem as overwhelming.

This is where you can kick it into high gear and teach him to RETHINK that he's never stuck unless he CHOOSES to think, act or feel stuck. Let him know that, whether he thinks he can't or thinks he can, he's right. It's his thinking that will help him either solve a problem or keep it.

Take the problem(s) he's experiencing and help him break them down into small, simple, RETHINKING CHOICES, he has complete CONTROL over making. Explain to him that making these simple choices will bring him one step closer to solving the problem. Help him further understand the benefit of PROCESS thinking by asking: *"Will making these smaller step-by-step choices be a better option than choosing to stay stuck?"*

Reinforce to him that: 1) The only people without problems are dead! 2) The world is filled with jerks, and 3) In a tornado; even a turkey can fly. This should influence him into RETHINKING the choices made up to this point, where he wants to go, and the PROCESS steps he can choose to get there. Just helping him step back and RETHINK is a move in the right direction.

Understanding that you may have to continue to reinforce and repeat what you're saying is part of life as a parent. Sometimes your kids just need to know you care, that you understand where they are, and that you know they have the power, control and choice to move forward. Just keep thinking of yourself as the one who's throwing salt in the horse's oats.

High School

Typical Problem:
"I've had a major breakdown in relationship with my child over the past few months. I try to talk with her and she refuses. All she does is roll her eyes, turn her back to me, or just walk away and mumble. I feel like I want to just grab her and throttle her. Help!"

Practical Solution:
This used to really bug me! When I asked a question and someone didn't answer, I just about blew a gasket! NOT anymore. Step back, RETHINK, focus on this as an OPPORTUNITY to assess yourself, your RELATION-SHIP with your child, and your home environment.

One set of parents attempted to control their son's unruly behavior by removing his bedroom door and placing a mattress on the floor, providing only minimal food, and refusing to talk to him. In response, the young man attempted to CONTROL his parents controlling him by choosing to turn up his stereo, sing loudly and prance around naked in his room.

His parents viewed him as a nut! They wanted him locked up or "fixed," as they put it. When I asked them to take an inventory of what they were doing, they became defensive and refused to believe THEY had any responsibility for his behavior.

I see this quite often. The parents believe it's the kid's fault entirely. When I ask kids what they gain from these types of behaviors, they often say, *"It works."* According to one young man, *"It drove them nuts!"* He went on to say, *"My parents can't stand it when they don't see something affecting me the way they want it to. My way of controlling works better than theirs, I'm even having Fun!"*

Passive-aggressive behavior, like refusing to talk, rolling the eyes, walking away, and the like, are all "flags or flares" in the air, indicating that you need to focus on the areas of CONTROL, CHOICES, RELATIONSHIP, and NEEDS within *The Eight Areas of The Power of Productive Choices.*

It's inventory time for you, to see if *you* are providing an opportunity for your daughter to: 1) talk openly; 2) demonstrate her trustworthiness; 3) allow for the expression of her feelings; and 4) allow her to demonstrate her loyalty to the family structure.

By and large, children who choose passive-aggressive behavior perceive problems in many of these four areas between themselves and their parents. Asking your daughter to help you assess how she thinks *you* are doing in these four areas will reap a great reward in the long run. She'll immediately see you're not placing blame on her, but rather trying to better understand what the problem is.

If she perceives you as a NEED fulfilling person in her life, she'll move toward you. If she perceives you as NEED reducing, she'll move away. It's as simple as that. The bottom line is that building a RELATIONSHIP with your daughter when you're dealing with these passive-aggressive behaviors will take time.

If you're a PROCESS-thinking parent, you understand this. If you're focused on the OUTCOME of having your child answer your questions right now, behave better right now, then good luck! Call me when the smoke clears and we'll talk about YOUR choices.

Chapter 11

Yats Esool

Massive success begins with knowing that YOUR ATTITUDE REALLY IS EVERYTHING. Seize each day with a passion to be the greatest parent ever!

Yats Esool

We found out early in this book that many people around the world are asking similar questions: What's going on with our kids today, compared to when I grew up? What happened? The choices kids are making today are light years away from the choices made on the old planet. As a result, many parents are looking for a strategy to save their sanity—or what's left of it.

We also found out that nobody gave us a manual when we entered into the world of parenting. As stated before, you get more instructions with a new microwave than you do with parenting. Learning through experience or "on the job experience" becomes many parents' best choice at the time. Because you have kids, you will have problems. Hopefully, we've provided you with a different set of lenses through which to view those problems.

We found out that the kids on this "new planet" say things like, *"So."* *"Whatever." "That's cool." "You can do what you want because I'm not going to change!"* With these changes came an attitude of "demandingness," in the form of a "me" attitude or an "I-don't-care-about-anyone-but-myself" attitude, leading to the common middle name of "get me, buy me, take me, give me."

We've found that what kids really want is more responsibility for their own lives and more independence from others. Along with this, they want to make their own decisions. They want to take effective control of their own lives and take on that responsibility. They want to have power in their own lives. And last but not least, we found they want to make their own choices and not be controlled by adults.

They hate rigidity via rules and restrictions, but want structure laid down from us in a caring, calm tone of voice. They want to be talked with, not screamed at. They want to be allowed to demonstrate trust, as well as express their feelings, without being put down.

We found out that Pogo, the "philosopher," might have been right when he said, *"We have met the enemy and they is us."* It's healthy for us to look at what part of the problem we own. By starting with ourselves, we can begin to put the rethinking skills outlined in this book to work in our own lives first, and then teach and model them to our kids.

Let me share with you a final but important story that really stays with me every day of my life. It's a story I believe will stay with you as well. My first professional colleague, Al Lehrke, a marine veteran and assistant principal at the high school where I was serving in Austin, Minnesota, taught me some interesting things during the years we worked together.

One such lesson involved a phrase I often heard him use. From the first day we met, he had called me "Tommy," which was just fine with me. As I'd leave school each day, Mr. Lehrke would lean around the corner of his office and shout out, "Tommy, Yats Esool!"

I'd just say goodbye and be on my way, wondering what the heck he was saying to me. He repeated it day in and day out. One day, I stopped and asked him what it meant. But he just kept saying "Yats Esool," and telling me to figure it out.

Well, being the impatient person I was back then, I wanted the answer *right now!* I didn't want to take the time to "figure it out!" Finally, one day, after begging him to tell me the secret, Mr. Lehrke showed me a plaque with the words YATS ESOOL on it. "Spell it backward," he said, and walked out the door.

I stood in his office, looking at the plaque like a monkey trying to do a math problem, until I finally figured it out. Sure enough, when you spell YATS ESOOL backward, it spells STAY LOOSE.

Yats Esool, Mr. Lehrke. Yats Esool, everyone!

SUGGESTED PURCHASE LIST

Below you will find a listing of books that I strongly recommend to you in your search for continued growth and knowledge. They are excellent resources for your personal and professional library.

Applegate, Gary. *Happiness: It's Your Choice.* Berringer Publishing. 1989.

Burns, David. *Feeling Good: The new mood therapy.* New York: William Morrow and Co., Inc. 1980.

Ellis, Albert and Harper, Harper, Robert. *A New Guide To Rational Living.* Wilshire Book Company. 1975.

Faber, Adele & Mazlish, Elaine. *How To Talk So Kids Will Listen & Listen So Kids Will Talk.* Avon Books, 1980.

Ford, Edward E.
  Choosing To Love, 1983.
  Love Guaranteed, 1979.
  Freedom From Stress, 1989, 1993.
  Discipline For Home And School, Book One, 1994, 1995, 1997, 2003.
  Discipline For Home And School, Book Two, 1996, 1999.

Glasser, William.
  Reality Therapy. New York: Harper & Row, 1965.
  Take Effective Control Of Your Life. New York: Harper & Row, 1985.
  Control Theory In The Classroom. New York: Harper & Row, 1986.

Glenn, H. Stephen & Nelsen, Jane. *Raising Children For Success.* Sunrise Press. 1987

Hansen, Mark Victor.
  Chicken Soup for the Soul. Health Communications, Inc. 1996
  The One Minute Millionaire. Harmony Books. 2002.

Helmstetter, Shad. *Predictive Parenting.* Pocket Books. 1989

Maultsby, Maxie. *Help Yourself To Happiness.* New York: Institute For Rational Living, Inc. 1975.

Powers, W.T.
  Behavior: The Control Of Perception. Chicago: Aldine. 1973.
  Making Sense of Behavior: The Meaning of Control, Benchmark Publications. 1998.

Tartaglia, Louis A. *Flawless!* Eagle Brook. 1999.